FLORENCE'S
GLASSWARE
Pattern
IDENTIFICATION GUIDE
VOLUME II

Easy Identification for
GLASSWARE
from 1900
through the 1960s

COLLECTOR BOOKS
A Division of Schroeder Publishing Co., Inc.

On the Cover:

Rosalind, Tiffin Glass Company

Lois, Tiffin Glass Company

Hummingbird with Roses, Consolidated Lamp & Glass Company

Cover design by Beth Summers
Book design by Holly C. Long

Searching for a Publisher?

We are always looking for knowledgeable people considered to be experts within their fields. If you feel that there is a real need for a book on your collectible subject and have a large comprehensive collection, contact Collector Books.

Collector Books
P.O. Box 3009
Paducah, Kentucky 42002 – 3009

www.collectorbooks.com

Gene Florence
P.O. Box 22185   P.O. Box 64
Lexington, KY 40522   Astatula, FL 34705

Acknowledgments

As always, there are numerous people to thank who went out of their way to help with the book. However, in this particular instance, Charley Lynch, the photographer, needs to be singled out. Imagine sitting in a photographer's lair, day in and day out, surrounded by stacks of boxes of glass that need to be photographed exquisitely, item by item. Imagine a hundred other interruptions a day, all requiring you to set aside what you're trying to accomplish in order to meet an impossible photography deadline because nearly every other phase of the work is awaiting your results. Think about having to put aside the whole task to take whole days out to photograph something else that is suddenly an even greater priority. Somehow, he accomplished this Herculean task! My editor remarked that the finished pieces lined out on studio tables began to make the place look like a huge garage sale!

I need, also, to thank readers and fellow dealers who wrote or e-mailed after the first book with exceedingly encouraging remarks — and questions about how soon I could do another one! That gave us (my wife, Cathy, and me) the incentive to actively look for items to include in a possible second volume. One dealer at a show specifically sought me out to tell me I had saved him "untold hours" of research. Another remarked that a book of this type had been needed for a long time.

I thank Dick and Pat Spencer who brought glass to the studio and Arlyn Ols, who walked up to Cathy at a show and handed her a piece of glass "to photograph for the next Pattern ID book." I thank the dealer who sat down with us and implored us to "name" things that previously had been identified only by a factory number "so the collector and dealer have a label to 'hang onto' when shopping the markets." I had been very reluctant to do that in the past. We made every effort to find whatever names the collectors had already been using for the glass herein, however. Often there is an unofficial name already in use; these have always been put in quotation marks so you can tell it is not an official name given by the factory.

I thank my wife, who not only helped spot items for the book but who spent untold hours, again, surrounded by books, magazines, and newspaper articles searching for whatever bits of information she could find on a piece of glass I'd purchased. She, then, took over putting it on the computer when my seemingly smooth three book schedule suddenly turned into five in the same time frame, plus ten seminars that mushroomed out of the two initially discussed. Cathy even went so far as to dig out materials from storage which I had purchased over a 30-year span believing they would yield data; and they did — albeit slowly, after hours of pouring through them! I should note that not every scrap of information gleaned from sources I own were documented for the already too long bibliography; however, we tried to be diligent in acknowledging the information from any other author's work. We also tried to find at least two sources for the information presented here. Often there were more than that and very often they did not completely agree. There were a few exceptions where only one source could be found; and in a few cases, the items area is merely our best estimate, not concrete fact.

I need to thank my son, Marc, who solved numerous computer "glitches" for me and for Cathy, who is being forced to learn "computer-ese." He had to give some crash sessions, and, in a few cases, perform some tricky maneuvers himself to save her time. There was an Apple computer repairman who unlocked my jammed computer at a crucial ninth hour when the tech support system couldn't. Sorry, I don't remember what his name was, but that does not in any way diminish my gratitude for his help.

Thanks to my mother and father-in-law, Sibyl and Charles Gaines, who helped pack glass and record photo information both before and after the photography sessions. There cannot be enough said of their willing support and helpfulness in all aspects of our busy lives.

Thanks go to the usual support from the staff at Collector Books, up to and including Billy Schroeder himself who pitched in to label pictures as deadlines pressed near.

Much gratitude goes to you, the buying public, who graciously supported my efforts on the first book. I hope this second one finds you equally receptive.

The goal for this book was to give a quick reference to pattern identification of things you run into in the various market places, today. Admittedly, in the first book we used some pictures we already had of patterns that had appeared in some of the 64 books on glass that I have written over the past 30 years; but the goal was the same, to quickly identify patterns for collectors. Once a pattern name is known, one can either stop with that information or carry research further. I can't tell you the hours I've spent in books absolutely frustrated trying to find certain patterns. Some collectors don't want to know more than a name for the item they inherited from grandmother. For those who require a bit more, we tried to give a quick run down of who made it, when first made, plus colors it could be found in and, where known, the number of items manufactured. This seemed a simple format. You would not believe the hours it has taken to glean just those few quick items; however, we hope it to be a beneficial expenditure of our time. You should know that some companies reissued their wares, off and on, throughout their life span in same or different colors and pieces.

This particular second edition was to have included only items from the various markets we visited in the last two years, so you could have a feel for what is still available there. We believe that goal is at least 98 percent met. Somehow a few pictures came up missing and, at the last minute, we had to substitute a few from past books. Even so, we consciously tried not to duplicate anything shown in the first book, even though we stumbled onto some better shots that begged including! In an instance or two, an etch may be repeated from the first book, but the blank on which the etch appears is different. The second goal was to not rehash first book information. If you missed the first edition, you should get it soon before it goes out of print. Books, today, have a one or two year "life" in book stores; after that, you have to find them on secondary markets at increased prices.

We also set monetary goals on the items shown. A large percentage of what is shown was purchased for $20 or less. I keep hearing that you cannot find anything "good" in the marketplace anymore. We did not find that to be true.

Another goal for these books was to show a kind of historical perspective of glass made over the past hundred years, much of which can still be gathered today for either use or "shelf enjoyment." A separate factor in the mix was the glass needed to be representative of the various factories, great or small, who mostly are no longer in business! Let's face it, the very fact of their demise lends a certain immediate collectibility to their glassware!

That brings up another issue in the glass collecting world. Very often, at a factory's end, their molds for glass move onward to another company. The second, or third, company may reissue glass from the older molds. Since a number of the "founding father" glass companies have fled the scene in the last 20 years, it's natural that we are seeing glass on the market from these "reissues." Reproduction has been an especially negative word for collectors since they usually deflate prices on increasingly pricey collectibles. However, reissues of glass have been a standard in the glass companies' repertoires since their beginning. Every national "birthday" period, centennial, sesquicentennial, bicentennial, has seen reissues of "historical" glass products and during the thirties and forties you could find numerous advertisements selling wares as "fine reproductions of older glass patterns," be they their own past wares or someone else's. A few factories built their reputations entirely upon owning older molds and producing new products from them. So, I think we as collectors and lovers of glass need, perhaps, to be a little less condescending in our attitudes toward such reissues since these wares may have merit in the hazy future of glass.

Having said that, I need to go to the other side and say I have little patience with the rip-off artists who import glassware from cheaper overseas markets for the express purpose of "fooling" the buying public into thinking they are getting an antique. Indeed, there has been talk in collecting circles lately of petitioning Congress to require imprinted dates on glass being manufactured to stop this practice. If you are buying glass for investment, you need to keep yourself informed. If you buy glass because it appeals to you and "old or new, you just love it," as one lady put it, then all you need do is enjoy it! After all, that is the point where most of us started.

PATTERN NAME: ACANTHUS, ETCH #282,
STEM #5098 REG. OPTIC
Company: Fostoria Glass Co.
Years: c. 1930
Colors: amber and green with crystal
Items: 80+

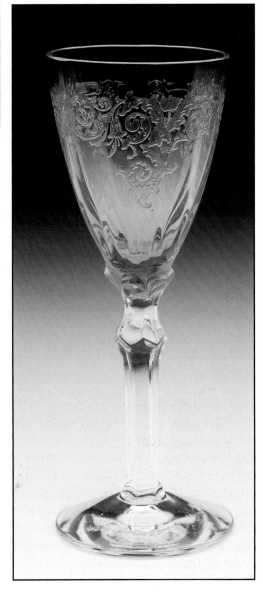

PATTERN NAME: "ACORN," NO. 130
Company: A.H. Heisey & Co.
Years: c. 1929
Colors: crystal, Moongleam (green), Flamingo (pink)
Items: 1

PATTERN NAME: ADAM, #730
Company: Morgantown Glass Works
Years: c. 1918
Colors: crystal
Items: 10+

PATTERN NAME: "ADAM'S RIB," LINE #900
Company: Diamond Glass Co.
Years: c. 1925
Colors: blue, green, iridized, marigold,
              milk glass
Items: 17+

PATTERN NAME: ADAM-SIERRA
Company: Jeannette Glass Co.
Years: c. 1930
Colors: pink
Items: 1 top; could appear on
           two different bottoms

PATTERN NAME: ADAMS, STEMWARE LINE #7390
Company: Cambridge Glass Company
Years: c. 1920s
Colors: crystal
Items: 30+

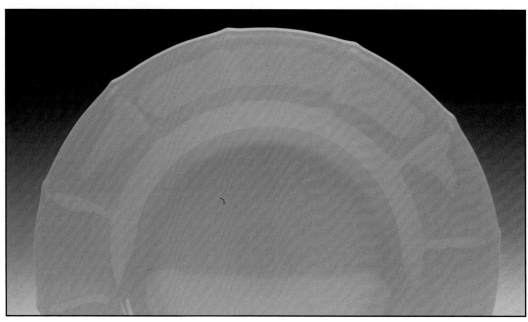

PATTERN NAME: "ADDIE," LINE #34, ALSO "12 POINT RIM"
Company: New Martinsville Glass Mfg. Co.
Years: c. 1930
Colors: black, crystal with black, jade green, green, pink, cobalt, ruby, and with silver rim

PATTERN NAME: ADONIS, #720; BLANK 3500/113
Company: Cambridge Glass Co.
Years: c. 1927
Colors: crystal
Items: 25+

PATTERN NAME: ALAHAMBRA
Company: Tiffin Glass Co.; U.S. Glass Co.
Years: c. 1930s
Colors: crystal, mandarin with crystal,
rose with crystal
Items: 65+

PATTERN NAME: ALEXIS #1630
Company: Fostoria Glass Co.
Years: c. 1909
Colors: Crystal
Items: 40+

9

PATTERN NAME: AMAZON, SAWTOOTH BAND
Company: U.S. Glass Co.
Years: c. 1890
Colors: crystal, crystal with ruby stain
Items: 28+

PATTERN NAME: AMBASSADOR ETCH,
              GASCONY #3397 BLANK
Company: A.H. Heisey & Co.
Years: c. 1932
Colors: Crystal, Sahara
Items: 15

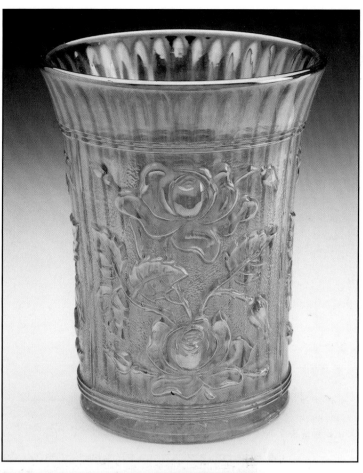

PATTERN NAME: AMERICAN BEAUTY
                    ROSE, #489
Company: Imperial Glass Co.
Years: c. 1909
Colors: iridescent azure, helios,
             rubigold, crystal satin, milk
             glass, nugreen, pink satin,
             vaseline, pink carnival
Items: 8+

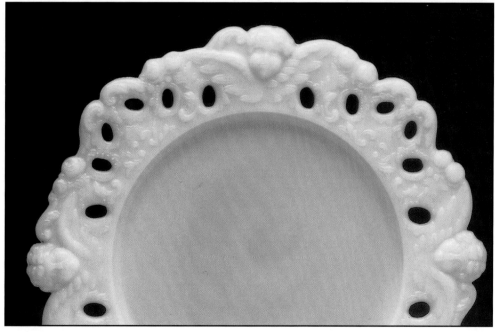

PATTERN NAME: "ANGEL HEAD"
Company: Westmoreland Glass Co.; John E. Kemple Glass Works
Years: c. 1950s
Colors: milk glass
Items: 1

PATTERN NAME: ARBOR ROSE, CUT #982
Company: Glastonbury
Years: c. 1950s
Colors: crystal

PATTERN NAME: "ARCADIA LACE,"
ROSE BAND, LINE #202
Company: Portland Glass Co.;
Jenkins Glass Co.
Years: c. 1927
Colors: Crystal
Items: 22+

PATTERN NAME: ARCHED OVALS
Company: U.S. Glass Co.
Years: c. 1905
Colors: crystal, crystal with ruby stain
Items: 20+

PATTERN NAME: ARLINGTON
Company: Anchor Hocking Glass Corp.
Years: c. 1986
Colors: crystal
Items: 2

PATTERN NAME: ASTER CUT #114
Company: Imperial Glass Co.
Years: c. 1918
Colors: Crystal
Items: 14+

PATTERN NAME: ATHENA, "PANELED 44,"
                            "REVERSE 44"
Company: U.S. Glass Co.
Years: c. 1912
Colors: crystal, crystal with ruby
Items: 15+

PATTERN NAME: ATHENS-DIANA
                            (PLATINUM RIM)
Company: Tiffin Glass Co.
Years: c. 1931
Colors: Crystal, Mandarin with gold
Items: 40

PATTERN NAME: ATHLONE, #17301
Company: Tiffin Glass Company
Years: c. 1950
Colors: Crystal
Items: 5

PATTERN NAME: AUTUMN
Company: McKee Glass Co.
Years: 1934
Colors: French Ivory, Jade Green, black
Items: 2

PATTERN NAME: AZTEC ROSE, #3125
Company: Jeannette Glass Co.
Years: c. 1950s
Colors: Flashed red, blue, Shell Pink, crystal
Items: 1

PATTERN NAME: "BALL & RIB," #5075
Company: Anchor Hocking Glass Corp.
Years: c. 1940s
Colors: crystal
Items: 2+

PATTERN NAME: "BALL & SWIRL," SWIRL & BALL #1842
Company: Westmoreland Glass Co.
Years: 1940s; 1960s
Colors: crystal; amber, amethyst, blue, crystal, green slag, milk glass, red and purple carnival, cerise, crystal with ruby flash
Items: 180+

PATTERN NAME: BAMBOO OPTIC, OCTAGON
Company: The Liberty Glass Works
Years: c. 1929
Colors: pink, green
Items: 12

PATTERN NAME: BAMBOO OPTIC, ROUND
Company: The Liberty Glass Works
Years: 1929
Colors: crystal, green, pink
Items: 7+

PATTERN NAME: "BANANA FRUITS"
Company: Duncan & Miller?; Indiana Glass Co.
Years: c. 1930s; 1960s
Colors: crystal with stains
Items: 8+

PATTERN NAME: "BANDS & PUNTIES,"
                      CUT #3001
Company: Anchor Hocking Glass Corp.
               (Standard Glass Co.)
Years: 1930s and 1940s
Colors: crystal
Items: 18

PATTERN NAME: BANQUET #74,
                      "THUMBPRINT BLOCK"
Company: Columbia Glass Co.;
               Federal Glass Co.
Years: c. 1890s; 1914
Colors: crystal
Items: 15+

PATTERN NAME: BASKETWEAVE
Company: Fenton Art Glass
Years: c. 1911; 1970s
Colors: crystal, black, green
               opalescent, ruby,
               jade
Items: 5

PATTERN NAME: BEACON, CUT #767
Company: Fostoria Glass Co.
Years: c. 1937
Colors: crystal
Items: 44

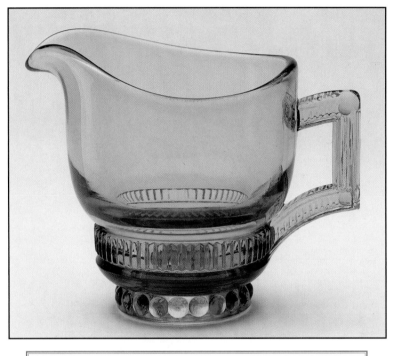

PATTERN NAME: "BEAD & FILE," LINE #330
Company: Canton Glass Co.
Years: c. 1954
Colors: Crystal, red, black, green, blue, amber
Items: 24

PATTERN NAME: BEADED PANEL AND SUNBURST, #1235
Company: A.H. Heisey & Co.
Years: c. 1897
Colors: crystal, crystal with decorations
Items: 60

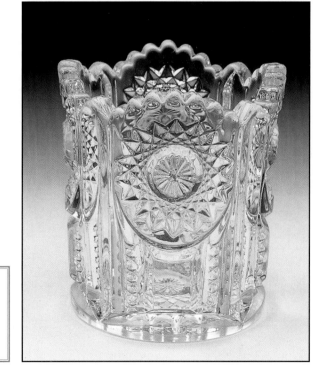

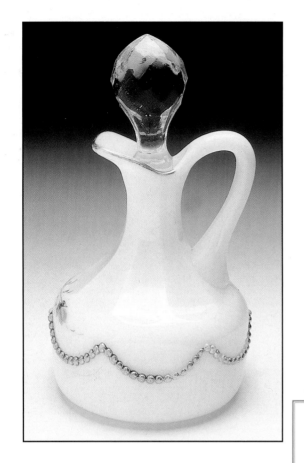

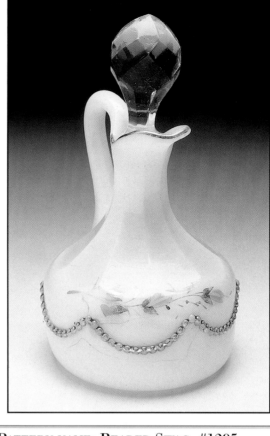

PATTERN NAME: BEADED SWAG, #1295
Company: A. H. Heisey & Co.
Years: c. 1898
Colors: crystal, Moongleam, milk glass
           with gold
Items: 30

PATTERN NAME: BEADED SWIRL, #335
Company: George Duncan & Son; U.S.
         Glass Co.
Years: c. 1880s; 1891
Colors: crystal, emerald, green,
           gold trims, milk glass
Items: 15

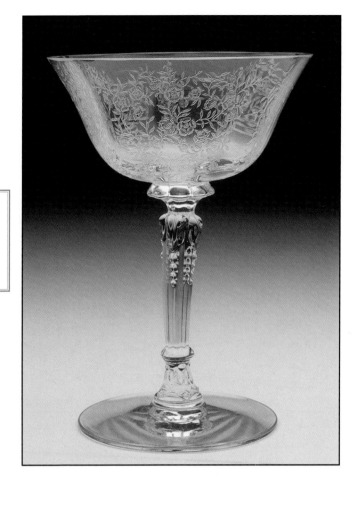

PATTERN NAME: BELLE-LE-ROSE, QUEEN
ANNE STEM #5009
Company: A. H. Heisey & Co.
Years: c. 1934
Colors: crystal

PATTERN NAME: "BELLFLOWERS
THREE" (THREE
FLOWERS),
SPRINGTIME
(MEDALLION)
Company: Lotus Glass Co.
Years: c. 1930s
Colors: crystal, crystal with gold,
pink, green, milk glass
with black
Items: 1+

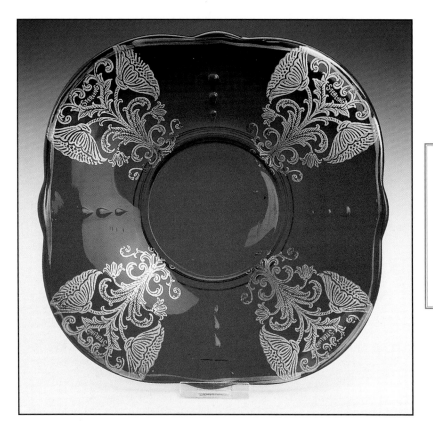

PATTERN NAME: "BELLFLOWERS TWO"
(ETCH), CROW'S
FOOT SQUARE BLANK
#412
Company: Lotus Glass Co.?;
Paden City Glass Mfg. Co.
Years: c. 1930s
Colors: red, yellow, crystal, cobalt

PATTERN NAME: BERRY, "SEASHELL," "BARBERRY"
Company: Boston & Sandwich; McKee & Brothers
Years: 1860s; c. 1880
Colors: crystal
Items: 30+

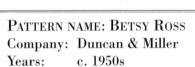

PATTERN NAME: BETSY ROSS
Company: Duncan & Miller
Years: c. 1950s
Colors: milk glass
Items: 17

PATTERN NAME: BEVERLY #276, #5097
                    TWIST STEM
Company: Fostoria Glass Co.
Years: c. 1927
Colors: azur, amber, green, orchid,
               amber with crystal, green
               with crystal
Items: 80+

PATTERN NAME: "BIRDS AND BRANCHES,"
                    ETCH, GLADES LINE #215
Company: Paden City Glass Mfg. Co.;
               Canton Glass Co.
Years: c. 1930s; 1950s
Colors: Crystal with satin
Items: 19+

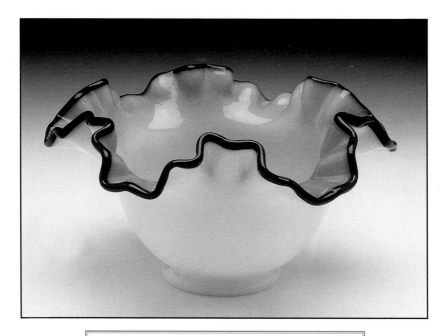

PATTERN NAME: BLACK ROSE
Company: Fenton Art Glass
Years: c. 1953; hand vase 1992, 1997
Colors: pink with black crest
Items: 10

PATTERN NAME: "BLAISE," "SCROLLED THISTLE," LINE #705
Company: Imperial Glass Co.
Colors: #40 amber, #81 green, #91 pink, crystal
Items: 1

PATTERN NAME: BLOCK & FAN
Company: U.S. Glass Co.
Years: c. 1891
Colors: crystal, opal, ruby stain
Items: 5+

PATTERN NAME: BLUE BIRD
                #103, BIRD &
                STRAWBERRY
                #157
Company: Indiana Glass Co.
Years: c. 1980s; 1914
Colors: blue, cobalt; crystal

PATTERN NAME: "BONITA," COIN
                GOLD DECORATION
Company: Bonita Art Glass Co.
Years: c. 1922
Colors: Green band decoration
          with 22k gold

PATTERN NAME: BORDETTE
DECORATION,
OXFORD BLANK
Company: Corning Glass Works;
Macbeth-Evans Division
Corning Glass Works
Years: c. 1940
Colors: pink, green, blue, yellow

PATTERN NAME: "BOUQUET & TASSEL,"
DEEP PLATE ETCH
#701, #3051 BLANK
Company: Cambridge Glass Co.
Years: c. 1927
Colors: crystal, crystal with gold
Items: 21

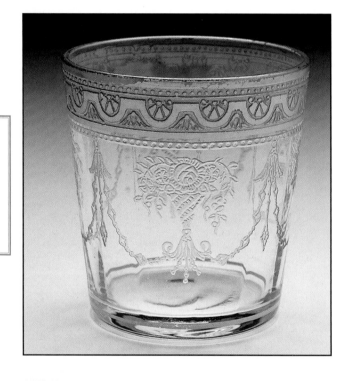

PATTERN NAME: "BRAMBLE ROSE,"
ETCH #743
Company: Morgantown Glass Works
Years: c. 1931
Colors: Crystal
Items: 12+

PATTERN NAME: BREAKFAST BOWL,
                    #8133
Company: Tiffin Glass Co.
Years: c. 1924
Colors: green, pink
Items: 1

PATTERN NAME: BRIDAL BOUQUET, ETCH
                 #0906; #1503 PADEN CITY
                 CANDLE BLANK
Company: Glastonbury Lotus
Years: c. 1930s
Colors: Crystal; crystal with gold
Items: 15+

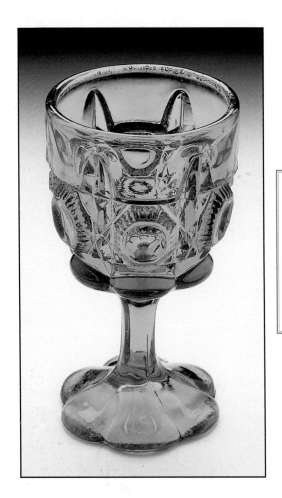

PATTERN NAME: BULL'S EYE AND DAISY, LINE #15117;
        #818
Company: U.S. Glass Co.; Kanawha Glass Co.
Years: c. 1910; 1974
Colors: crystal, crystal with amethyst or blue or green
       or pink or ruby trim; amber, blue, canary,
       milk glass
Items: 9+; 1

PATTERN NAME: BUTTERFLY, DECORATION
        #508; MAYFAIR BLANK #2419
Company: Fostoria Glass Co.
Years: c. 1931
Colors: Topaz with black enamel
Items: 11

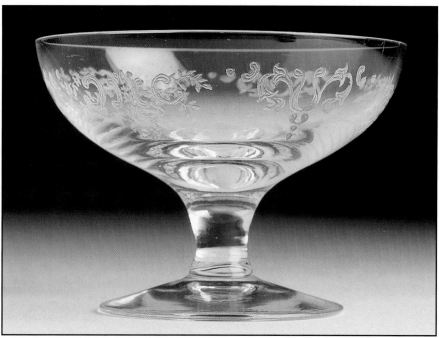

PATTERN NAME: "C.E. GARLAND," ETCH #210
Company: Fostoria Glass Co.
Years: c. 1910
Colors: crystal
Items: 90

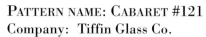

PATTERN NAME: CABARET #121
Company: Tiffin Glass Co.
Colors: pink

PATTERN NAME: "CABLE," LINE #378
Company: Lancaster Glass Co.
Years: c. 1930s
Colors: rose, topaz
Items: 2

29

PATTERN NAME: CAMEO DIAMOND #1011,
                    CAMEO DECAGON
Company: Westmoreland Glass Co.
Years: c. 1930
Colors: pink and "all popular colors"
Items: 8

PATTERN NAME: "CAMPANULA"
Colors: crystal, crystal with
              ruby stain

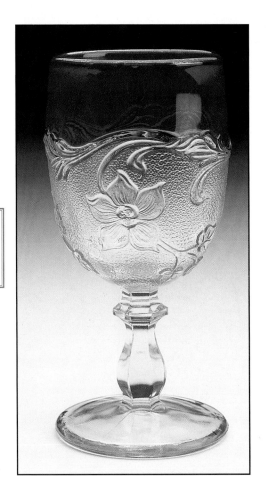

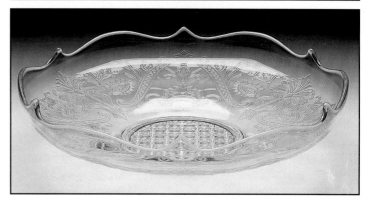

PATTERN NAME: "CANE LANDRUM," #765
Company: Lancaster Glass Co.
Years: c. 1932
Colors: topaz, pink
Items: 4

PATTERN NAME: CARLTON, ETCH #778;
#7606½ ATHENA STEM
Company: Morgantown Glass Works
Years: c. 1931
Colors: crystal with cased ebony
filament stem
Items: 6

PATTERN NAME: CARLTON, ETCH #778;
                MONTGOMERY WARD'S "MILAN"
Company: Morgantown Glass Works
Years: c. 1931
Colors: Crystal
Items: 8

PATTERN NAME: CELESTIAL
Company: Fostoria Glass Co.
Years: c. 1985
Colors: crystal, blue, sun gold
           with iridescence
Items: 5

PATTERN NAME: CHANTILLY
Company: Jeannette Glass Co.
Years: c. 1960
Colors: crystal
Items: 5

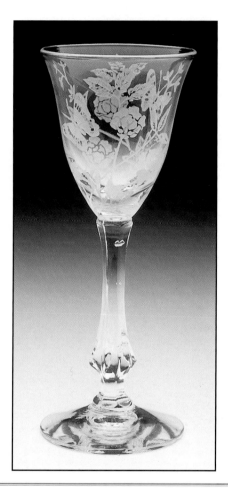

PATTERN NAME: CHARMAINE ROSE ETCH;
DIAMOND #5375 STEM
Company: Duncan & Miller
Years: c. 1950s
Colors: crystal
Items: 26

PATTERN NAME: CHARMAIN
Company: Tiffin Glass Co.
Years: c. 1930s
Colors: Crystal, amber, amber with gold
Items: 16+

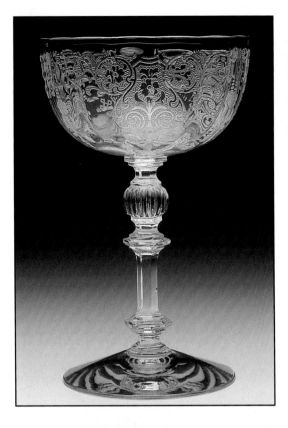

PATTERN NAME: CHATEAU, ETCH #315;
"JEWEL" STEM #6008
Company: Fostoria Glass Co.
Years: c. 1933
Colors: Crystal
Items: 19

PATTERN NAME: CHECKERBOARD, LINE #500;
OLD QUILT (IN MILK GLASS)
Company: Westmoreland Glass Co.
Years: c. 1912; 1940s; 1970s
Colors: crystal, crystal with gold; milk glass;
           carnival, green, several blues, purple
           marble, and with paint decorations
Items: 70+

PATTERN NAME: "CHECKERED QUESTIONS,"
SAND BLAST ETCH #682
Company: Tiffin Glass Co.
Years: c. 1915
Colors: Crystal
Items: 13

PATTERN NAME: CHRISTIANA, CUT
#814, STEM #6030
Company: Fostoria Glass Co.
Years: c. 1942
Colors: crystal
Items: 12

PATTERN NAME: CHROMA #123, CORONET (1937),
VICTORIAN (1941)
Company: Imperial Glass Co.
Years: c. 1957
Colors: crystal, ruby, burgundy, evergreen,
indigo, madeira, custard
Items: 8

PATTERN NAME: CLASSIC, "RACHEL" IN ROYAL RUBY
Company: Anchor Hocking Glass Corp.
Years: c. 1940s; 1963
Colors: Royal Ruby; Anchorwhite, and with gold, crystal
Items: 7

PATTERN NAME: "CIRCLES"
Company: McDonald Glassworks, Inc.
Years: late 1920s
Colors: pink, green, crystal, lustre

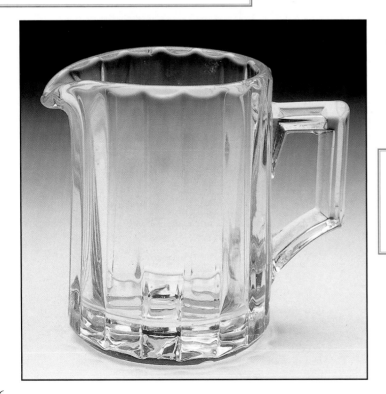

PATTERN NAME: "COARSE RIB," #407
Company: A.H. Heisey & Co.
Years: c. 1923
Colors: crystal, Flamingo, Moongleam
Items: 39

PATTERN NAME: COINSPOT;
                 CONCAVE COLUMN,
                 LINE #617
Company: National Glass Co.;
          Dugan Glass Co.
Years: c. 1901
Colors: white; blue, green, canary
Items: 4

PATTERN NAME: COLONIAL
                 CRYSTAL,
                 "CHESTERFIELD
                 LINE" #600
Company: Imperial Glass Co.
Years: c. 1920s
Colors: Teal, White, Blue,
          Marigold, Clambroth,
          Smoke, red, crystal
Items: 30+

PATTERN NAME: COLONIAL DESIGN
Company: L.E. Smith Glass Co.
Years: c. 1932
Colors: Black with crystal

PATTERN NAME: COLONIAL LADY
Company: Anchor Hocking Glass Corp.
Years: c. 1954
Colors: crystal with white, green with white
Items: 6

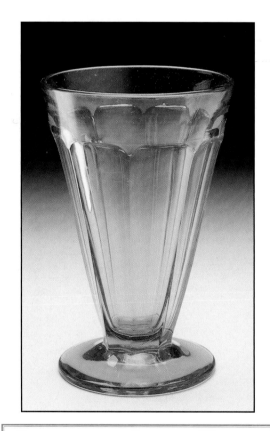

PATTERN NAME: COLONIAL (MEDIUM
          FLAT PANEL), #353
Company: A.H. Heisey & Co.
Years: c. 1906
Colors: amber, crystal
Items: 90+

PATTERN NAME: COLONIAL PRISM #2183; CENTENNIAL II (1970s)
Company: Fostoria Glass Co.
Years: 1920; 1970s (three pieces)
Colors: Crystal, amber, blue, green, canary, orchid, azure, rose

PATTERN NAME: COLONIAL WITH GARLAND, "FERN GARLAND"
Company: McKee Brothers Glass Co.
Years: c. 1895
Colors: Crystal
Items: 16+

PATTERN NAME: CONSTELLATION WITH
GRAPE #0753
Company: Indiana Glass Co.
Years: c. 1972
Colors: Crystal
Items: 1

PATTERN NAME: CORALBEL
Company: Duncan & Miller
Years: c. 1950s
Colors: crystal
Items: 8+

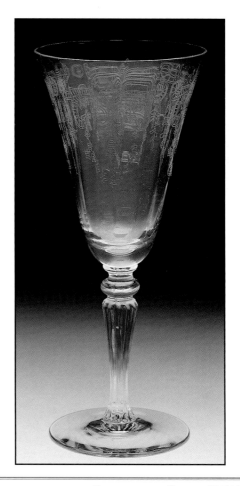

PATTERN NAME: CORONADA, STEM #15071
Company: Tiffin Glass Co.
Years: 1932
Colors: crystal, crystal with mandarin
Items: 40+

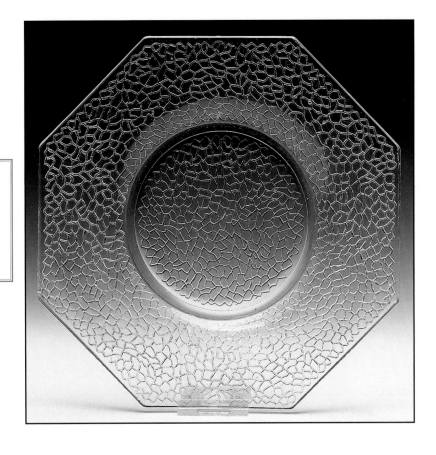

PATTERN NAME: "CRACKLE," #100
Company: L.E. Smith Glass Co.
Years: c. 1925
Colors: amber, crystal, canary, green
Items: 9+

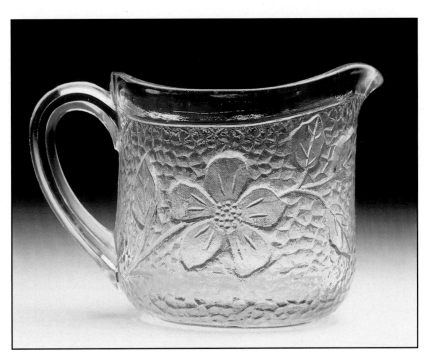

PATTERN NAME: "CRACKLED BLOSSOM"
Company: U.S. Glass Co.
Years: c. 1920s
Colors: pink
Items: 2

PATTERN NAME: CRINKLE (TRANSPARENT);
EL MEXICANO (OPAQUE)
Company: Carbone; Morgantown
Glass Works
Years: c. 1962; c. 1940s
Colors: amethyst, ruby, peacock blue,
green, pink, topaz, crystal,
white, black, moss green, blue,
amberina, steel blue; ice,
seaweed, pink quartz, hyacinth
Items: 18+

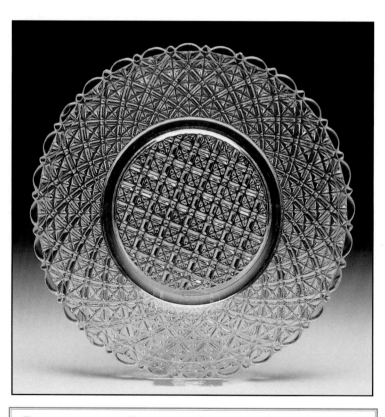

PATTERN NAME: CRUSADER CROSS OR STAR; FINE CUT
Company: Bryce Brothers; U.S. Glass Co.
Years: c. 1880s
Colors: Crystal; canary; blue, amber
Items: 9+

PATTERN NAME: CUPID'S HART (DEER), CUPID'S HUNT
Years: c. 1880s
Colors: crystal
Items: 6+

PATTERN NAME: CUT #484
Company: Seneca Class Co.

PATTERN NAME: CUT #1288
Company: Seneca Class Co.
Colors: crystal

PATTERN NAME: CUT WILD ROSE,
                         LINE #3200
Company: Cambridge Glass Co.
Years: 1920s
Colors: crystal, red
Items: 19

PATTERN NAME: DAHLIA #131
Company: Indiana Glass Co.
Colors: Crystal and with goofus
                decoration
Items: 6

PATTERN NAME: "DAHLIA," LINE #286
Company: D. C. Jenkins Glass Co.
Years: 1929
Colors: Green
Items: 21

PATTERN NAME: DAISY & BUTTON
WITH NARCISSUS
#124; "CLEAR LILY"
Company: Indiana Glass Co.
Years: c. 1925
Colors: crystal, crystal with gold
and with colors
Items: 16+

PATTERN NAME: DAISY & BUTTON WITH
                  THUMBPRINT & PANEL
Company: Adams & Co.; U.S. Glass Co.;
                L.G. Wright Glass Co.
Years: 1886; 1890s; 1930s
Colors: amber, canary, blue, red
Items: 10+; 3

PATTERN NAME: DAISY & BUTTON WITH V
Company: A.J. Beatty & Sons; U.S. Glass
                Co.; L.G. Wright Glass Co.
Years: c. 1885; 1892; 1970s
Colors: crystal; amber, blue canary,
                apple green

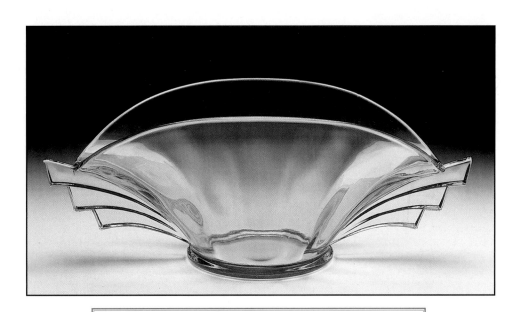

PATTERN NAME: DEAUVILLE, #3125 STEMWARE
                            (DESIGN MOULDED INTO STEM)
Company: Cambridge Glass Co.
Years: c. 1931
Colors: Gold Krystol
Items: 4

PATTERN NAME: "DECO," NO. 16
Company: Duncan & Miller
Years: c. 1930s
Colors: Pink, crystal, green, black, red, cobalt
Items: 2

PATTERN NAME: DEEP ETCH #36
Company: H.C. Fry Glass Co.
Years: c. 1920s
Colors: crystal
Items: 15+

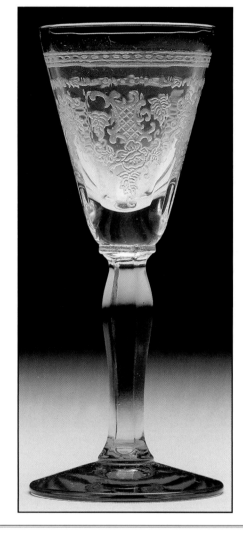

PATTERN NAME: DELPHIAN, ETCH #272;
           BLANK #5082
Company: Fostoria Glass Co.
Years: c. 1925
Colors: Crystal with blue
Items: 42

PATTERN NAME: DEUX COQS, "COCK-A-TWO,"
           #733 ETCH; STEM #3120
Company: Cambridge Glass Co.
Years: 1927
Colors: Blue, green, crystal
Items: 20+

PATTERN NAME: DEW & RAINDROP #50
(OLD STRAIGHT STEM)
Company: Kokomo Glass Mfg. Co.;
Federal Glass Co.?
Years: c. 1905; 1930s
Colors: crystal, crystal with ruby
flash and gold; amber, blue
Items: 13

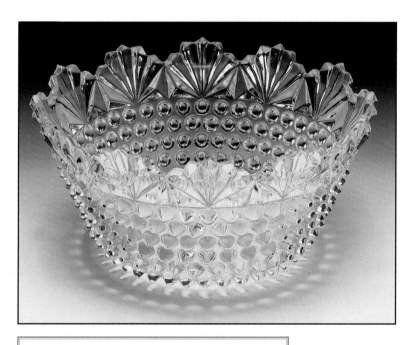

PATTERN NAME: "DEWDROP 'N FAN,"
EARLY AMERICAN
HOBNAIL #641
Company: Imperial Glass Co.
Years: 1930s; 1965; 1980s
Colors: crystal, opalescent, brown,
blue, ruby
Items: 12+

PATTERN NAME: "DIADEM" #2430
Company: Fostoria Glass Co.
Years: 1929
Colors: rose, azure, green,
amber, ebony, crystal,
topaz
Items: 5

PATTERN NAME: DIAGONAL BAND, "BLOCK & FAN"
Company: U.S. Glass Co.
Years: c. 1891
Colors: crystal
Items: 9+

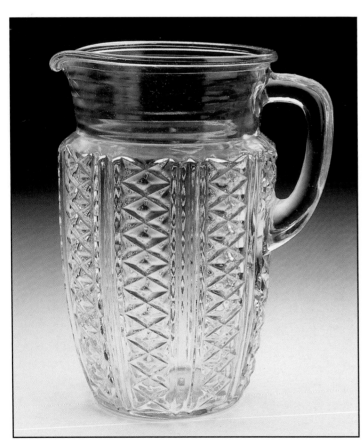

PATTERN NAME: DIAMOND
Company: Anchor Hocking Glass Corp.
Years: c. 1941
Colors: crystal
Items: 5

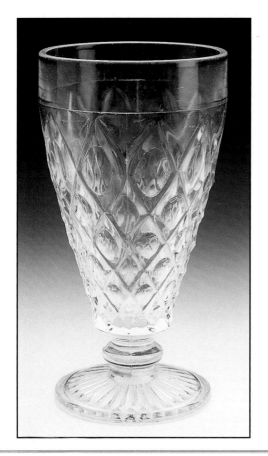

PATTERN NAME: "DIAMOND & THUMBPRINT"
Company: Hazel Atlas Glass Co.
Years: 1936
Colors: Crystal, pink
Items: 4

PATTERN NAME: DIAMOND #5375 STEM
Company: Duncan & Miller
Colors: crystal

PATTERN NAME: DIAMOND #75
Company: Duncan & Miller
Colors: Crystal, crystal with gold
Items: 54+

PATTERN NAME: DIAMOND CRYSTAL #7019
Company: A. H. Heisey & Co.
Colors: Crystal
Items: 2

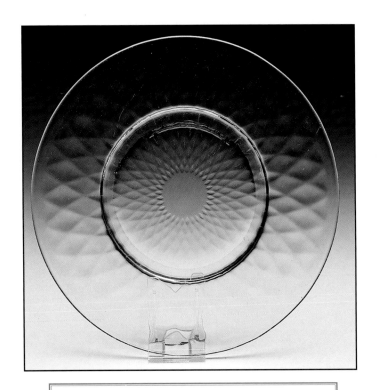

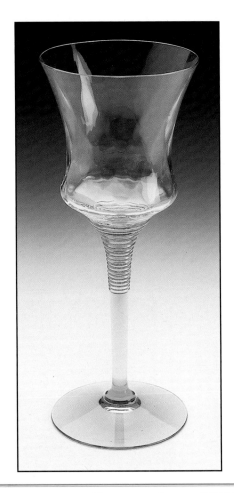

PATTERN NAME: DIAMOND OPTIC, #1502
Company: Fenton Art Glass
Years: c. 1927
Colors: green, pink, jade, aqua, black,
           orange, red, pearl
Items: 60+

PATTERN NAME: DIAMOND OPTIC #3370,
               AFRICAN STEM
Company: A.H. Heisey & Co.
Years: c. 1924
Colors: crystal with moonglcam
Items: 1

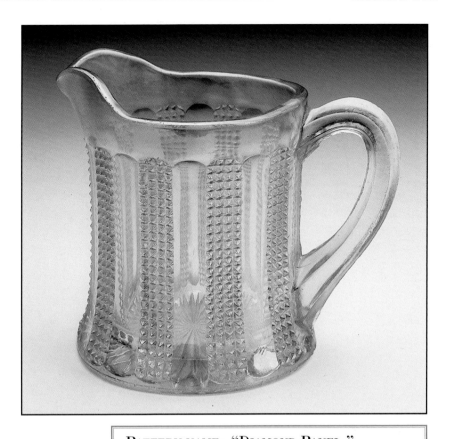

PATTERN NAME: "DIAMOND PANEL,"
                    "DIAMOND POINT COLUMNS"
Years: c. 1920s
Colors: crystal, green, marigold, pink
Items: 6

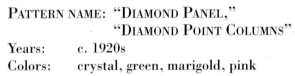

PATTERN NAME: DIAMOND PEG
Company: McKee & Brothers;
            Jefferson Glass Co.
Years: c. 1895; 1913
Colors: custard, green with gold,
            crystal with ruby
Items: 10+

PATTERN NAME: DIAMOND SUNBURST #2711/680 (CREAMER)
Company: Fostoria Glass Co.
Years: c. 1958
Colors: white, Aqua, Peach Milk Glass
Items: 4

PATTERN NAME: DIVING GIRL, NO. 352
Company: The Phoenix Glass Co.
Years: c. 1947
Colors: blue, yellow
Items: 1

PATTERN NAME: DOLLY MADISON (SHAPE),
                    LINE #14179 CALLED NERISSA (WITH
                    STRAIGHT SIDE, OPTIC SHAPE #15041)
Company: Tiffin Glass Co.
Colors: crystal

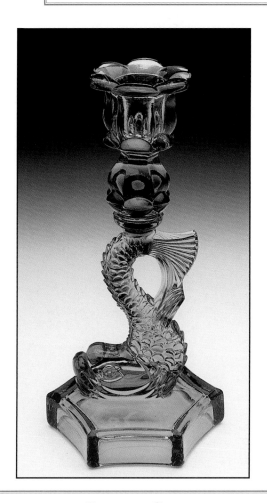

PATTERN NAME: DOLPHIN, CURVED
                   HEX BASE, #1049
Company: Westmoreland Glass Co.
Years: c. 1924; late 1970s
Colors: pink, green, crystal, opal, amber; milk
         glass, almond mist, antique blue, black
Items: 6

PATTERN NAME: DOUBLE COLUMBINE, CUT 405
                   (WIDE OPTIC)
Company: Tiffin Glass Co.
Years: c. 1930
Colors: crystal, crystal with amber and green
Items: 30

PATTERN NAME: DRESDEN
Company: Cambridge Glass Co.
Years: c. 1922
Colors: crystal
Items: 30

PATTERN NAME: DRIFTWOOD CASUAL, #1980
Company: Seneca Glass Co.
Years: c. 1980
Colors: amber, accent red, yellow
buttercup, brown cinnamon,
Ritz or Peacock blue, Delphine
blue, grey, moss green, plum,
crystal
Items: 14

PATTERN NAME: "EGG HARBOR," "THUMBPRINT HANDLE"
Company: The Liberty Glass Works
Years: c. 1929
Colors: pink, green
Items: 9

PATTERN NAME: "EILEEN" NEEDLE ETCH #83,
            STEM #5082
Company: Fostoria Glass Co.
Years: 1928
Colors: green, pink, azure with crystal
Items: 20+

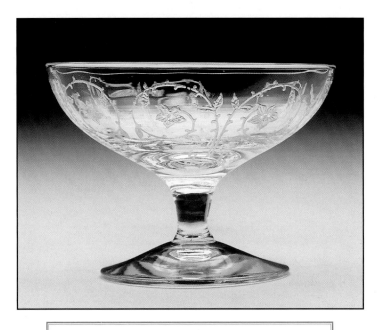

PATTERN NAME: "ENTWINED FLOWERS,"
            ETCH #212
Company: Fostoria Glass Co.
Years: 1910
Colors: crystal
Items: 110

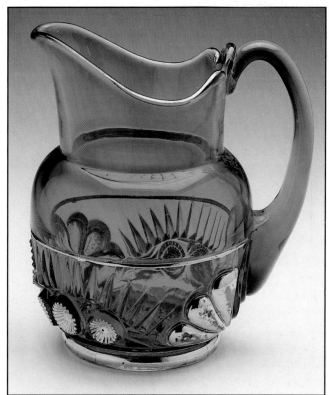

PATTERN NAME: ESTHER ("TOOTH & CLAW")
Company: Riverside Glass Works
Years: c. 1896
Colors: crystal, green with gold,
          ruby, amber stain
Items: 15

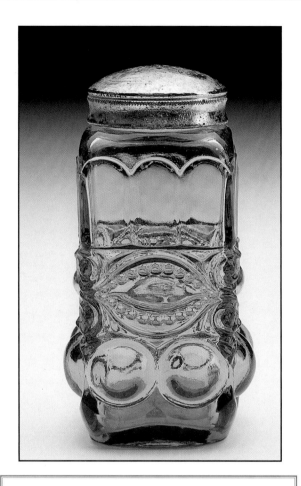

PATTERN NAME: ETHOL; OFTEN IDENTIFED AS
"CUT LOG"; CAT'S EYE &
BLOCK; NO. 15 PATTERN
Company: Bryce, Higbee & Co.; U.S. Glass Co.;
Westmoreland Glass Co.; Pioneer
Glass Co.
Years: 1889; 1892; 1902;
Colors: crystal
Items: 25

PATTERN NAME: "EYEWINKER," LINE #25
Company: L.G. Wright Glass Co.; Dalzell,
Gilmore & Leighton
Years: c. 1970; 1890
Colors: green, amber, crystal, ruby;
crystal
Items: 30 (new); 27 (old)

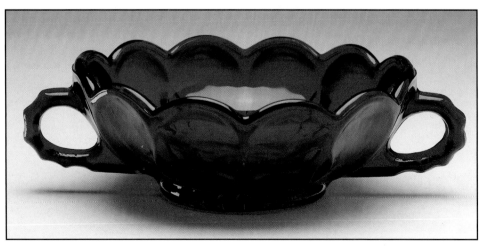

PATTERN NAME: FAIRFIELD
Company: Anchor Hocking
Glass Corp.
Years: 1970s
Colors: avocado, gold,
brown, blue, red

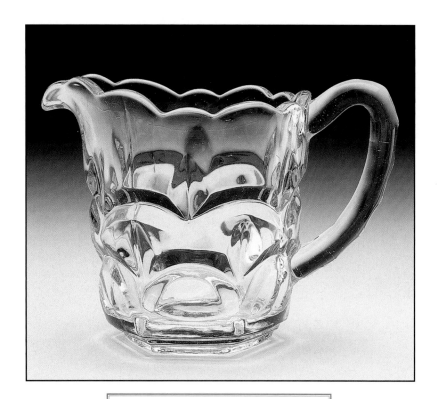

PATTERN NAME: FAKE HEISEY
Colors: crystal
Marking: H in diamond

PATTERN NAME: FAN, "DIAMOND D" DECORATION
Company: Dugan Glass Co.
Years: c. 1907
Colors: green, blue, ivory with gold
Items: 6

PATTERN NAME: "FANCY"
Company: Hazel Atlas Glass Co.
Years: c. 1929
Colors: green, crystal, pink,
cobalt, amethyst
Items: 4

PATTERN NAME: FANCY ARCH
Company: McKee Glass; John E. Kemple
Glass Works
Colors: Emerald Green, crystal with gold

PATTERN NAME: FANCY LOOP,
#1205
Company: A.H. Heisey & Co.
Years: c. 1896
Colors: crystal, emerald
with gold
Items: 100+

PATTERN NAME: FANDANGO, #1201
Company: A.H. Heisey & Co.
Years: c. 1896
Colors: crystal
Items: 80+

PATTERN NAME: FANTASIA
Company: Princess House
Years: late 1980s
Colors: Crystal, crystal with
satin
Items: 9

PATTERN NAME: FARBERWARE
Company: Farber Brothers (metal);
           Cambridge Glass Co. (glass inserts)
Years: c. 1940
Colors: amber, amethyst, Forest Green,
           Royal Blue, Dark Emerald, Carmen,
           crystal, ebony, milk glass

PATTERN NAME: FERN #1495
Company: A.H. Heisey & Co.
Years: c. 1937
Colors: crystal, zircon, dawn
Items: 24

PATTERN NAME: FIESTA RINGS
Company: Hocking Glass Co.
Years: c. 1938
Colors: Crystal with colored bands

PATTERN NAME: FILAGREE CORNFLOWER (SILVER)
Company: Dugan Glass Co.
Years: c. 1907
Colors: blue, green, ruby and ivory with silver
Items: 8

PATTERN NAME: FILAGREE, LINE #10
Company: Westmoreland Glass Co.
Years: 1900
Colors: crystal with gold or silver, some blue, pink, green
Items: 15

PATTERN NAME: FIRENZE, ETCH #775
Company: Cambridge Glass Co.
Years: c. 1937
Colors: Crystal
Items: 30+

PATTERN NAME: FIRST LOVE, ETCH; "THREE FEATHERS" BLANK
Company: Duncan & Miller
Years: 1937
Colors: crystal
Items: 214+

PATTERN NAME: FLANDERS, ETCH #1011
Company: Lotus Glass Co.
Years: c. 1930s
Colors: crystal, topaz
Items: 17

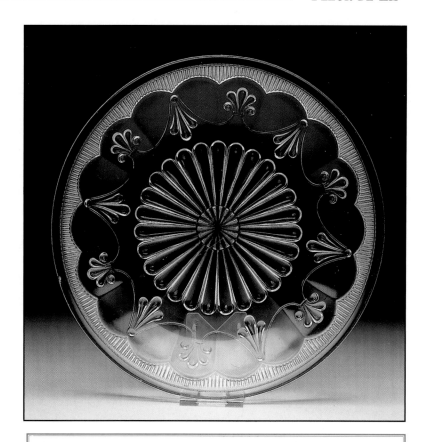

PATTERN NAME: FLEUR DE LIS & DRAPE (OR TASSEL); #15009
Company: Adams Co.; U.S. Glass Co.; Crystal Art Glass
Years: 1880s; 1890s; 1980s
Colors: emerald green; crystal, some milk glass; wine various colors
Items: 20+

PATTERN NAME: "FLEUR-DE-LIS" (HANDLE), #2331
Company: Fostoria Glass Co.
Years: 1926
Colors: blue, green, orchid
Items: 1

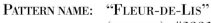

PATTERN NAME: "FLEUR-DE-LIS
SCROLL" ETCH;
NO. 12 BLANK
Company: Duncan & Miller
(blank)
Years: c. 1925
Colors: green, pink, cobalt,
ruby, crystal
Items: 2+

PATTERN NAME: "FLEUR-DE-LIS
SCROLLED," "IRIS
WITH MEANDER"
Company: Jefferson Glass Co.
Years: c. 1903
Colors: amber, amethyst, blue,
canary, crystal, green,
opalescent
Items: 14

PATTERN NAME: FLORA; OPPOSING PYRAMIDS
Company: Bryce, Higbee & Co.
Years: c. 1890
Colors: Crystal
Items: 11+

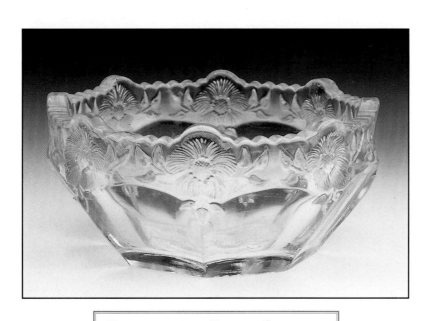

PATTERN NAME: FLORAL COLONIAL
Company: Westmoreland Glass Co.
Years: 1911
Colors: crystal
Items: 38

PATTERN NAME: "FLORAL GARLAND"
                ETCH, #1826
Company: Westmoreland Glass Co.
Years: 1932

PATTERN NAME: FLORAL PANEL; ROCK CRYSTAL #49
Company: New Martinsville Glass Mfg. Co.
Years: c. 1903
Colors: crystal, crystal with gold

PATTERN NAME: "FLORAL SHIELD,"
                 LINE #1000
Company: Tiffin Glass Co.
Colors: pink

PATTERN NAME: FLORET, ETCH #796
Company: Morgantown Glass Works
Years: c. 1932
Colors: crystal
Items: 6

PATTERN NAME: FLOWER BASKET
Company: H.C. Fry Glass Co.
Years: c. 1917
Colors: crystal
Items: 60+

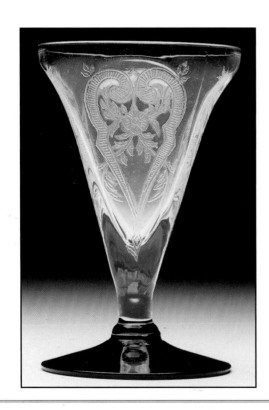

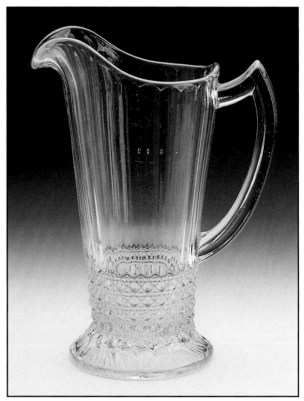

PATTERN NAME: "FLOWERING HEART,"
#741 ETCH
Company: Cambridge Glass Co.
Years: c. 1930s
Colors: crystal with black
Items: 10+

PATTERN NAME: "FLUTE & CANE,"
LINE #666½
Company: Imperial Glass Co.
Years: c. 1921; on/off through 1980s
Colors: crystal, marigold; green, light
blue, rose, caramel slag
Items: 27+

PATTERN NAME: FONTINELLE, ETCH #781;
                 #7673 LEXINGTON STEM
Company: Morgantown Glass Works
Years: c. 1931
Colors: crystal
Items: 7

PATTERN NAME: "FOX & HOUNDS,"
                 "WOODLANDS,"
                 #5097 BLANK
Company: Wheeling Decorating Co. (Etch)
           Fostoria Glass Co. (Blank)
Years: c. 1927
Colors: Crystal

PATTERN NAME: "FRANCES," LINE #2010
Company: Central Glass Works
Years: c. 1929
Colors: amber, green, rose
Items: 16+

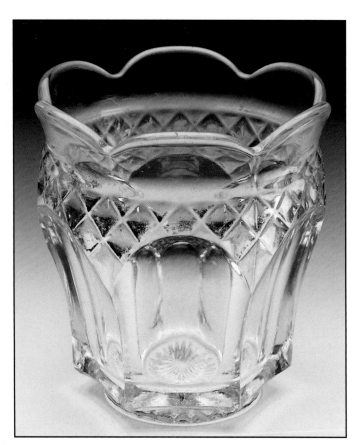

PATTERN NAME: FRONTIER, #C1761
Company: New Martinsville Glass Mfg. Co.
Years: c. 1912
Colors: crystal, crystal with gold or ruby
decoration
Items: 8+

PATTERN NAME: FROST,
ETCH #103,
"BEAD & FILE"
BLANK LINE
#330
Company: Paden City Glass
Mfg. Co.;
Canton Glass Co.
Years: 1920
Colors: crystal with "frost"
etch
Items: 10+

PATTERN NAME: GADROON, CUT 816; BLANK
#6030 ASTRID STEM
Company: Fostorial Glass Co.
Years: c. 1942
Colors: crystal
Items: 16

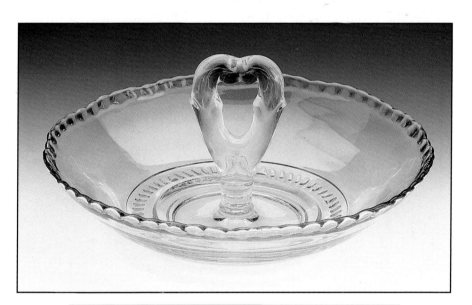

PATTERN NAME: GADROON, "ROPE," LINE #881
Company: Paden City Glass Mfg. Co.
Years: c. 1930s
Colors: yellow, red, cobalt, crystal

PATTERN NAME: GAELIC
Company: Indiana Glass Co.
Years: 1910
Colors: crystal and with
            decoration
Items: 15+

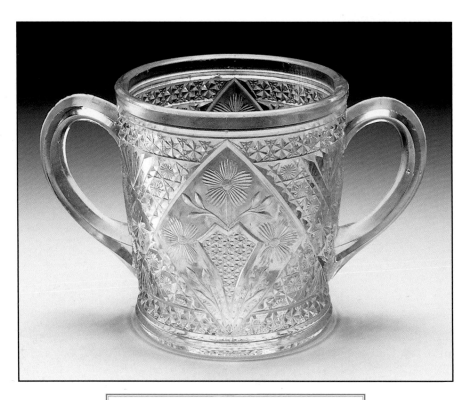

PATTERN NAME: GARDEN PINK #167
Company: Indiana Glass Co.
Years: 1913
Colors: crystal
Items: 1

PATTERN NAME: GARLAND, ETCH #237;
                 BLANK #880
Company: Fostoria Glass Co.
Years: 1915
Colors: Crystal
Items: 146

PATTERN NAME: "GEOMETRIC"
              LINE #2402
Company: Fostoria Glass Co.
Years: c. 1933
Colors: Amber, azure,
           crystal, ebony, green,
           rose
Items: 5

PATTERN NAME: GEORGIAN #1611
Company: Fenton Art Glass
Years: 1930; 1950s
Colors: amber, aqua, black,
           crystal, jade, green, pink,
           red, milk glass, cobalt
Items: 36

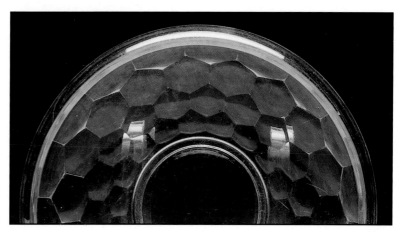

PATTERN NAME: GEORGIAN, LINE #103
Company: Duncan & Miller
Years: c. 1929
Colors: crystal, ruby, green, amber,
            blue, pink
Items: 25

PATTERN NAME: GIANT BULL'S EYE
Company: Bellaire Goblet Co.
Years: c. 1890s
Colors: Crystal
Items: 15+

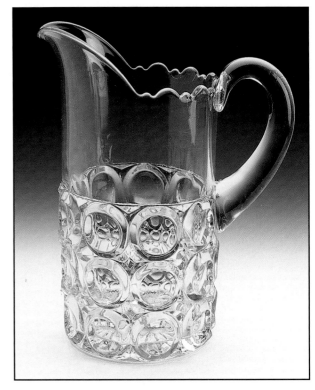

PATTERN NAME: "GOLD TRIANGLE,"
               "PAPER AEROPLANE"
               #2375½
Company: Fostoria Glass CO.
Years: c. 1930s
Colors: rose
Items: 2

PATTERN NAME: GOLDENROD
(WITH GOLD);
LAURELWOOD
(WITHOUT GOLD)
Company: Glastonbury Lotus
Years: c. 1930s
Colors: pink with gold, crystal with
gold

PATTERN NAME: GOLDWOOD, ETCH #264
(WOODLAND WITHOUT GOLD)
Company: Fostoria Glass Co.
Years: 1922
Colors: Crystal with gold
Items: 59

PATTERN NAME: "GOTHIC WINDOWS,"
              "GOTHIC ARCH," No. 166
Company: Indiana Glass Co.
Years: c. 1920
Colors: crystal
Items: 9+

PATTERN NAME: "GOLF SCENE"
Company: Cambridge Glass Co.
Years: c. 1929
Colors: green, blue, gold
          encrusted, pink
Items: 10+

PATTERN NAME: "GRACEFUL SATIN,"
              #1894/4
Company: Lancaster Glass Co.
Years: c. 1932
Colors: topaz and pink satin

PATTERN NAME: GRAPE CUT #1
Company: Standard Glass Mfg. Co.
Years: c. 1930
Colors: crystal, green, pink

PATTERN NAME: GRAPE CUT #6
Company: Standard Glass Mfg. Co.
Years: c. 1930
Colors: crystal, green, pink

PATTERN NAME: "GRAPE ON GRID," CUT #96
Company: Anchor Hocking Glass Corp.
               (Standard Glass Mfg. Co.)
Years: c. 1939
Colors: crystal
Items: 16

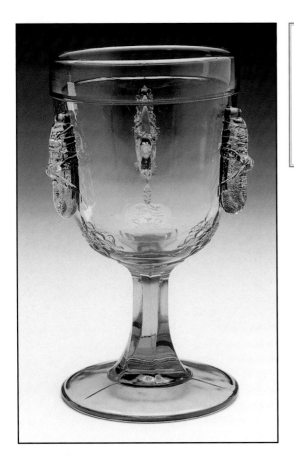

PATTERN NAME: "GRASSHOPPER,"
                 "LOCUST"; NO. 77-24
Company: Unidentified; L.G. Wright Glass Co.
Years: c. 1880s; 1970s
Colors: amber, blue, vaseline, crystal; amber,
          blue, crystal, green
Items: 15; 1

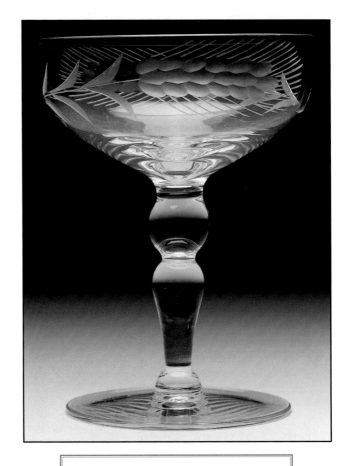

PATTERN NAME: GRAY WHEAT
Company: Glastonbury Lotus
Colors: crystal

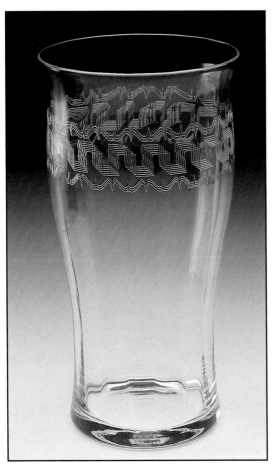

PATTERN NAME: GREEK DESIGN, NEEDLE ETCH #45
Company: Fostoria Glass Co.
Years: c. 1898; late 1920s
Colors: crystal with rose, green, amber; crystal
Items: 26

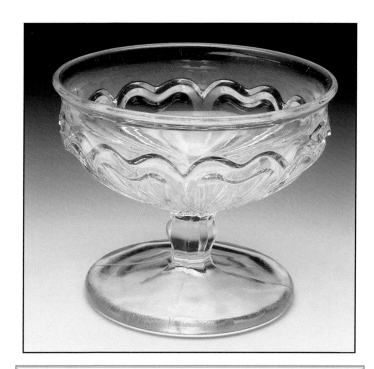

PATTERN NAME: GUERNSEY SEMI COLONIAL #2892
Company: Cambridge Glass Co.
Years: 1903
Colors: Crystal
Items: 30+

PATTERN NAME: GREEK ETCH; "HANGING
                STARS," #1241
Company: Central Glass Works
Colors: crystal
Items: 36

PATTERN NAME: "HALF TWIST,"
               STEM LINE #337
Company: Tiffin Glass Co.
Years: c. 1930s
Colors: crystal, crystal with black, rose

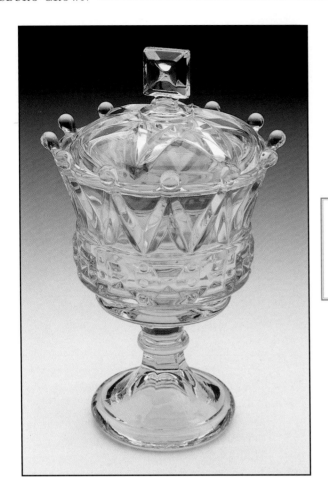

PATTERN NAME: HAPSBURG CROWN, #2750
Company: Fostoria Glass Co.
Years: 1961
Colors: Topaz, crystal, ruby, cobalt
Items: 4

PATTERN NAME: HAWAIIAN #2737
Company: Fostoria Glass Co.
Years: 1961
Colors: amber with brown, amber
          with peacock blue
Items: 14

PATTERN NAME: "HEART WITH
                  THUMBPRINT"
Company: Tarentum Glass Co.
Years: c. 1900
Colors: crystal with gold,
          green, custard
Items: 30

PATTERN NAME: HEAVY PINEAPPLE, #2000
Company: Fenton Art Glass
Years: c. 1938
Colors: rose and crystal satin; ruby; carnival
Items: 15

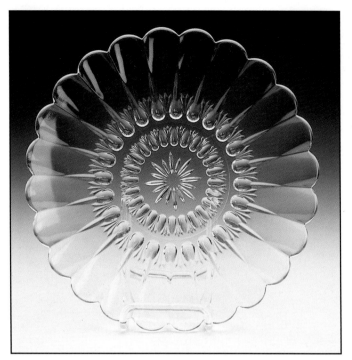

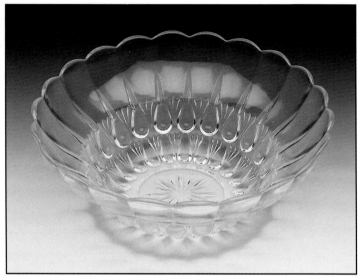

PATTERN NAME: HEIRLOOM #2435
Company: Federal
Years: 1956
Colors: crystal
Items: 5

PATTERN NAME: HEIRLOOM; CONTINENTAL,
          VICTORIAN, MARTHA WASHINGTON
Company: Cambridge Glass Co.
Years: 1950s; 1920s
Colors: crystal; amber, Royal blue, Forest
        green, ruby, Heatherbloom,
        milk glass
Items: 40+

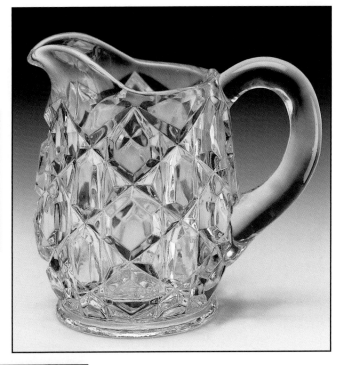

PATTERN NAME: Henrietta #14;
          "Big Block"
Company: Columbia Glass Co.;
          U.S. Glass Co.
Years: 1889; 1891
Colors: crystal, crystal with ruby stain
Items: 24+

PATTERN NAME: Heraldry,
          Cut #743;
          Contour
          Blank #2666
Company: Fostoria Glass Co.
Years: 1935; 1953
Colors: crystal
Items: 18

PATTERN NAME: "Herringbone,"
          #416
Company: A.H. Heisey & Co.
Years: c. 1919
Colors: pink
Items: 5

PATTERN NAME: "HEXAGONAL" FILAMENT STEM
Company: Morgantown Glass Works
Years: c. 1920s
Colors: Spanish Red, Stiegel Green, Ritz Blue, Ebony
Items: 6

PATTERN NAME: HIGH POINT, "SWORD
'N CIRCLE"
Company: Anchor Hocking Glass Corp.
Years: c. 1949
Colors: Crystal, Royal Ruby
Items: 5

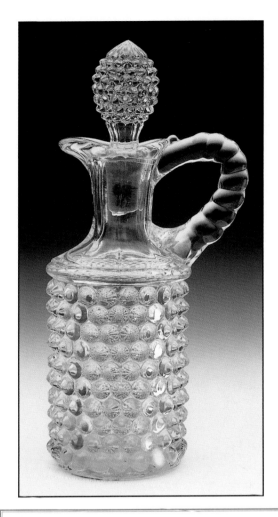

PATTERN NAME: "HONEYCOMB BAND," NEW YORK
Company: New Martinsville Glass Mfg. Co.; U.S. Glass Co.
Years: 1870s; 1890s
Colors: Crystal, crystal with ruby
Items: 6+

PATTERN NAME: HOBNAIL, "DEW DROP"
Company: Model Flint Glass Co.
Years: 1888
Colors: Crystal
Items: 12

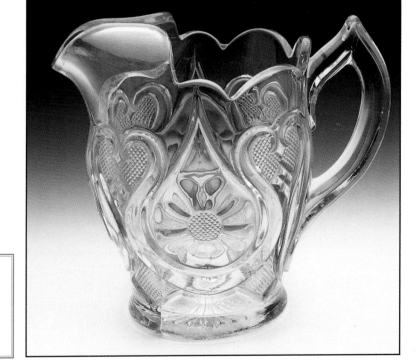

PATTERN NAME: HORSESHOE DAISY, #717
Company: New Martinsville Glass Mfg. Co.
Years: c. 1918
Colors: crystal
Items: 7+

PATTERN NAME: "HORSESHOE RIBBON,"
ETCH #601
Company: Tiffin Glass Co.
Colors: Crystal

PATTERN NAME: HUMMINGBIRD WITH ROSES
Company: Consolidated Lamp and Glass Co.
Years: c. 1930s
Colors: rare blue wash on crystal, purple

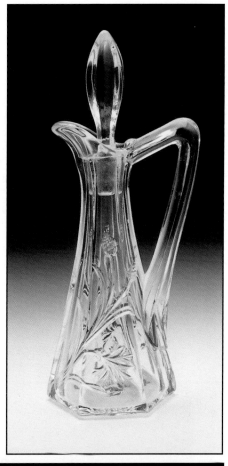

PATTERN NAME: I.C. PATTERN,
             "DANDELION," #1819
Company: Fostoria Glass Co.
Years: 1911
Colors: Crystal
Items: 56

PATTERN NAME: INDIANA, #15029, "PRISON WINDOW,"
             "FEATHER"
Company: U.S. Glass Co.
Years: c. 1896
Colors: crystal, crystal with gold

PATTERN NAME: INNOVATION #407
Company: McKee Glass Co.
Years: 1918
Colors: Crystal
Items: 13+

PATTERN NAME: INNOVATION, CUT
#1024; 98 BLANK
Company: McKee Glass Co.
Years: c. 1918
Colors: Crystal

PATTERN NAME: INNOVATION CUT #410
Company: McKee Glass Co.;
John E. Kemple Glass Works
Years: 1916; 1960s
Colors: crystal; blue, milk, Honey
amber
Items: 47

PATTERN NAME: INTAGLIO
Company: H. Northwood & Co.
Years: c. 1897
Colors: opalescent blue
Items: 12+

PATTERN NAME: INTAGLIO ROSE #698,
"WAFFLE" BLANK
Company: Imperial Glass Co.
Years: c. 1930s; 1950s
Colors: Crystal

PATTERN NAME: INTAGLIO
SUNFLOWER,
#15125
Company: U.S. Glass Co.
Years: c. 1911
Colors: crystal, crystal with
ruby trim
Items: 6+

PATTERN NAME: INTERPRETATION (DESIGNER COLLECTION)
Company: Fostoria Glass Co.
Years: c. 1977
Colors: opal, purple, crystal, brown
Items: 9

93

PATTERN NAME: JABOT
Colors: crystal
Items: 6

PATTERN NAME: JACOBEAN, LINE #15317
Company: U.S. Glass Co.
Years: c. 1920s
Colors: crystal, green, marigold
            iridescent, pink
Items: 2+

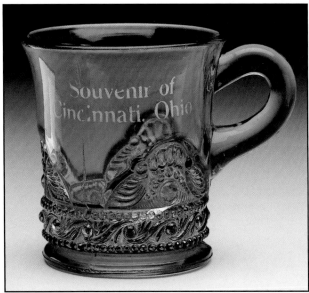

PATTERN NAME: JEWEL, COLORADO (WITH FEET),
                "LACY MEDALLION"
Company: U.S. Glass Co.; Crystal Art Glass;
          Summit Art Glass
Years: c. 1900s; 1960s; 1970s
Colors: crystal, emerald, crystal with ruby stain;
            crystal, cobalt blue, ruby; amber,
            crystal, green, blue
Items: 18+; 1; 2

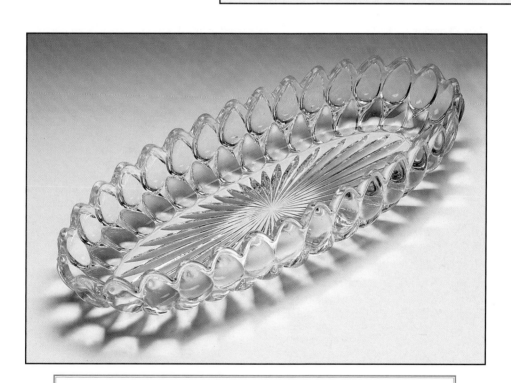

PATTERN NAME: "JEWELED BUTTERFLIES,"
MIKADO
Company: Indiana Glass Co.
Years: c. 1908
Colors: crystal, crystal with gold
Items: 15+

PATTERN NAME: "JOB'S TEARS" (MISTAKEN COMMON NAME),
TEARDROP ROW
Company: Bryce, Higbee & Co.
Years: c. 1899
Colors: Crystal
Items: 12+

PATTERN NAME: JOCKEY,
                STEM 3
Company: Morgantown
           Glass Works
Years: c. 1960s
Colors: crystal, crystal
           with amber stem
Items: 1

PATTERN NAME: KARNAK #4161
Company: Fostoria Glass Co.
Years: 1961
Colors: Smoke, Pine, Marine, Amber
Items: 5

PATTERN NAME: "KOKOMO," LINE #400
Company: D.C. Jenkins Glass Co.
Years: c. 1930
Colors: Crystal, Crystal with decorations
Items: 15+

PATTERN NAME: "KEY," ETCH #215
Company: Fostoria Glass Co.
Years: 1910
Colors: Crystal
Items: 95+

PATTERN NAME: LACE BOUQUET, #810
(SEAR'S "FLORENTINE")
Company: Morgantown Glass Works
(for Sears)
Years: c. 1943
Colors: crystal
Items: 6

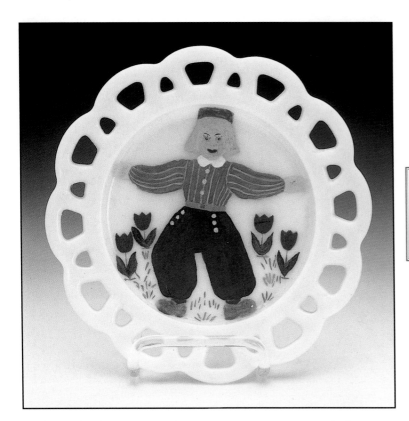

PATTERN NAME: LACE EDGE
Company: Anchor Hocking Glass Corp.
Years: 1940s
Colors: milk glass

PATTERN NAME: LACE EDGE
Company: Imperial Glass Co.
Years: c. 1956
Colors: milk glass

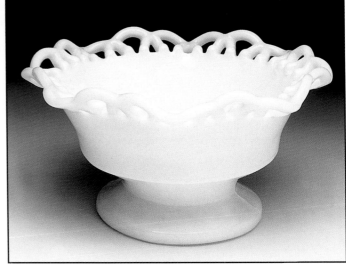

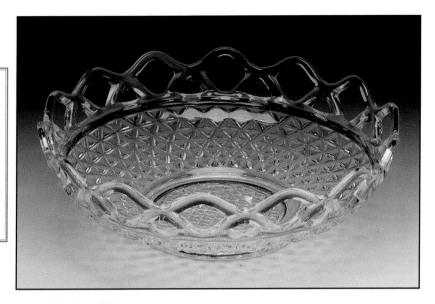

PATTERN NAME: LACE EDGE #749;
                "BELMONT CRYSTAL"
                #7497
Company: Imperial Glass Co.
Years: 1930s
Colors: crystal, blue; amber,
          burgundy, olive
Items: 20+

PATTERN NAME: "LACEY EDGE,"
               "LACEY CLUB"
Company: John E. Kemple Glass
          Works
Years: c. 1960
Colors: milk glass

PATTERN NAME: "LACY DEWDROP," "BEADED JEWEL"
Company: Cooperative Flint Glass Co.; Phoenix Glass Co.;
          John E. Kemple Glass Works; Wheaton
          Industries – Kemple Reproductions
Years: 1900s; 1937; 1940s; 1976
Colors: Blue, amber, crystal, green, milk glass,
          milk glass with blue
Items: 17

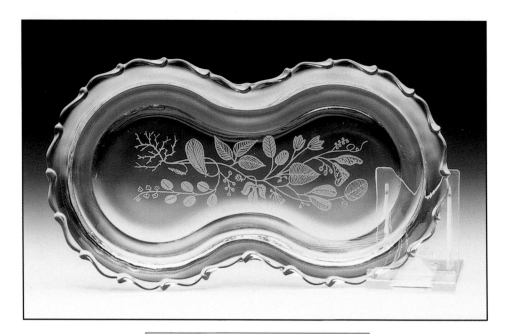

PATTERN NAME: LACY LEAF, #6
Company: Fostoria Glass Co.
Years: 1937
Colors: crystal
Items: 25

PATTERN NAME: LARCHMONT #1036
Company: Cambridge Glass Co.
Years: c. 1949
Colors: crystal
Items: 12+

PATTERN NAME: LARGE SUNBURST
          STAR; CUT 81
Company: Fostoria Glass Co.
Years: 1904
Colors: Crystal
Items: 270+

PATTERN NAME: LATTICE #321
Company: Cambridge Glass Co.

PATTERN NAME: LAUREL WITH BANDS, CUT #401
Company: Standard Glass Mfg. Co./
               Anchor Hocking Glass Corp.
Years: c. 1940
Colors: crystal
Items: 15

101

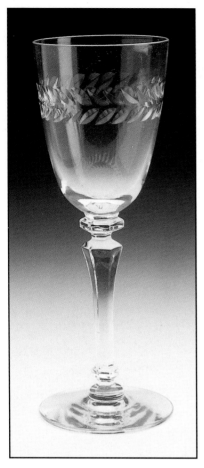

PATTERN NAME: LAURELWOOD ETCH/GOLDENROD (WITH GOLD)
Company: Glastonbury Lotus
Years: c.1930s
Colors: crystal, crystal with satin

PATTERN NAME: LAUREL WREATH,
                         #17361 STEM
Company: Tiffin Glass Co.
Colors: crystal

PATTERN NAME: "LEAF" #1200/4
Company: Anchor Hocking Glass Corp.
Years: c. 1942
Colors: crystal, Royal Ruby
Items: 2

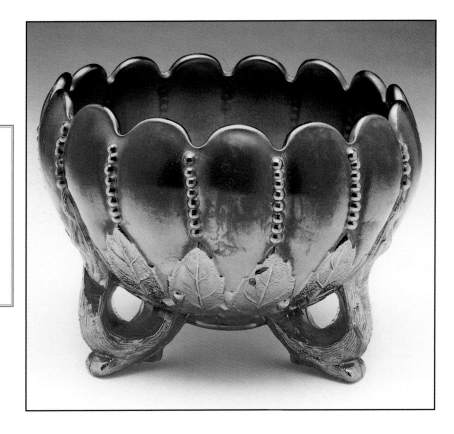

PATTERN NAME: LEAF AND BEADS,
"BEADED CABLE"
Company: H. Northwood & Co.;
Fenton Art Glass
Years: c. 1908; 1980s
Colors: crystal, opalesent,
carnival green, purple,
marigold
Items: 5

PATTERN NAME: "LEAF BAND,"
"LEAF"
Company: Macbeth-Evans,
Division Corning
Glass Works
Years: c. 1930
Colors: crystal, green, pink
Items: 1

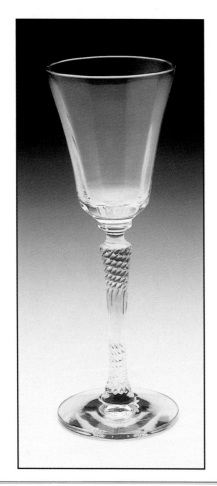

PATTERN NAME: LEGACY, #7654½
                WIDE OPTIC STEM
Company: Morgantown Glass Works
Years: c. 1930s
Colors: crystal, crystal with ebony
          or moonstone stem
Items: 6

PATTERN NAME: "LELA BIRD"
Company: Paden City Glass Mfg. Co.
Years: c. 1929
Colors: pink, green, black
Items: 12+

PATTERN NAME: LEXINGTON #758
Company: Cambridge Glass Co.
Years: 1934
Colors: crystal
Items: 13

PATTERN NAME: LIBERTY BELL
Company: Libbey
Years: c. 1973
Colors: crystal

PATTERN NAME: LILY OF THE VALLEY,
              ETCH #241;
              BLANK #858
Company: Fostoria Glass Co.
Years: c. 1916
Colors: Crystal
Items: 95+

PATTERN NAME: LINDA #17576
Company: Tiffin Glass Co.
Years: c. 1960s
Colors: Crystal
Items: 7+

PATTERN NAME: "LINDBURGH" #719
Company: Imperial Glass Co.
Years: c. 1930s
Colors: crystal, green, rose
Items: 16

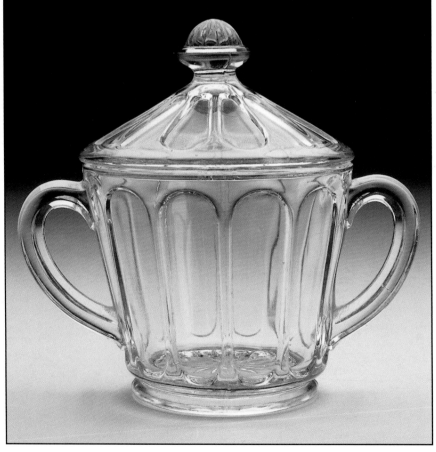

PATTERN NAME: LINE #115,
            "INDIANA SILVER"
Company: Indiana Glass Co.
Years: c. 1915
Colors: crystal, crystal with silver
          overlay
Items: 7+

PATTERN NAME: LINE #350; ETCH UNIDENTIFIED
Company: Bryce, Higbee & Co.
Years: c. 1916
Colors: Crystal
Items: 6

PATTERN NAME: LINE #444
Company: Paden City Glass Mfg. Co.;
              Canton Glass Co.
Years: c. 1930s; 1950s
Colors: crystal
Items: 19

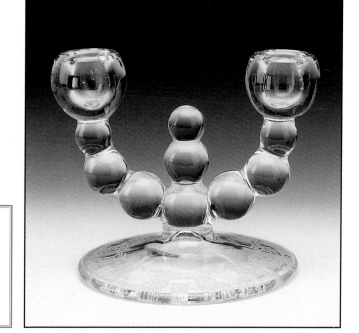

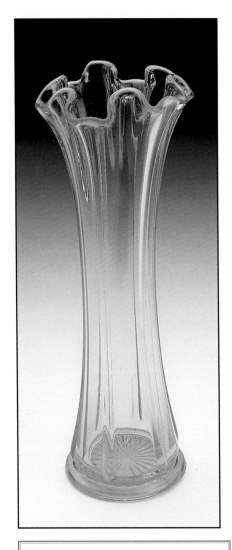

PATTERN NAME: LINE #3077; ETCH IMPERIAL HUNT SCENE #718
Company: Cambridge Glass Co.
Years: c. 1930s
Colors: amber, crystal, green, pink, blue, Madeira, Royal Blue, yellow, Midnight blue
Items: 15

PATTERN NAME: LINE #1510
Company: Imperial Glass Co.

PATTERN NAME: LINE #3088
Company: Anchor Hocking Glass Corp.
Years: c. 1942
Colors: pink, crystal
Items: 1

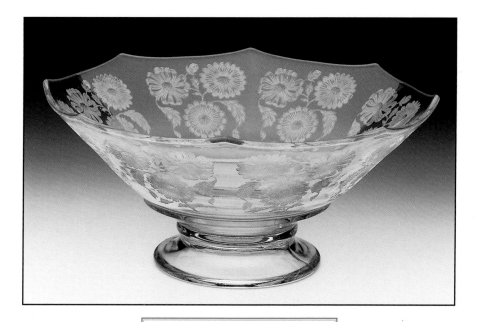

PATTERN NAME: LOIS
Company: Tiffin Glass Co.
Years: c. 1923
Colors: pink
Items: 16+

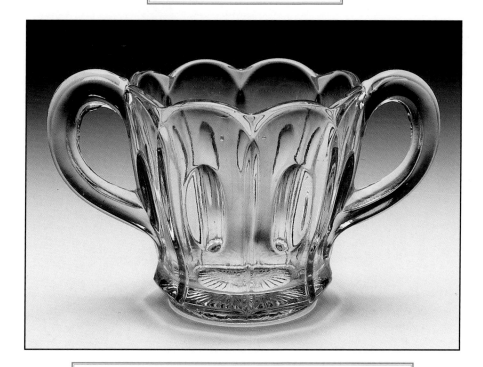

PATTERN NAME: "LONG THUMBPRINT"
Company: Diamond Glass Co.
Years: c. 1923
Colors: amethyst, blue, green, marigold, pink
Items: 5+

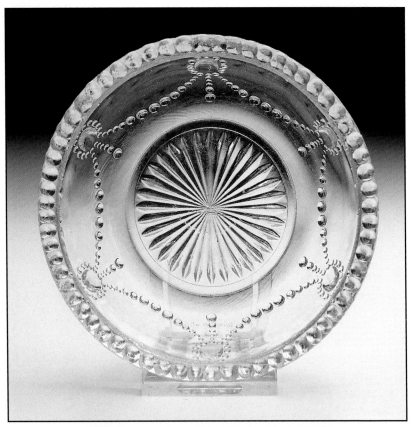

PATTERN NAME: LOOP & JEWEL;
                       JEWEL & FESTOON
Years: c. 1890
Colors: crystal
Items: 12+

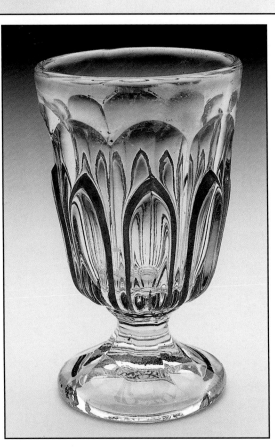

PATTERN NAME: LOOP & LONG PETAL
Colors: stains of red, yellow

PATTERN NAME: LOOP OPTIC (BOWL); #6014½
Company: Fostoria Glass Co.
Years: c. 1936
Colors: azur, crystal, Gold Tint
Items: 2

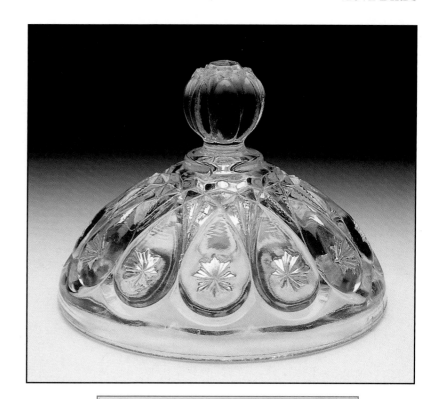

PATTERN NAME: LOOP OPTIC,
                LINE #4095
Company: Fostoria Glass Co.
Years: late 1920s
Colors: blue, green, amber foot;
            crystal, green spiral

PATTERN NAME: LOUISE, LINE #1121
Company: Fostoria Glass Co.
Years: 1902
Colors: crystal
Items: 30

PATTERN NAME: LOVE BIRDS
Company: Consolidated Lamp and Glass Co.
Years: c. 1940s?
Colors: White frost, crystal frost?
Items: 1

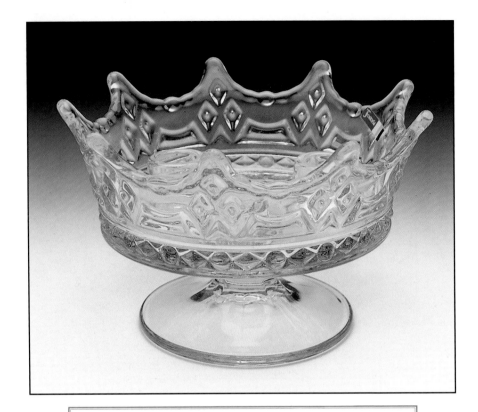

PATTERN NAME: LUXEMBURG, CROWN LINE #2766
Company: Fostoria Glass Co.
Years: c. 1963
Colors: Crystal, Royal Blue, Gold, Ruby
Items: 1

PATTERN NAME: MADEIRA, LINE 120-5
Company: Tiffin Glass Co.
Years: c. 1970
Colors: blue, citron, crystal, olive, smoke
Items: 6

PATTERN NAME: MAGNOLIA, #3790
SIMPLICITY STEM
Company: Cambridge Glass Co.
Years: c. 1950s
Colors: crystal
Items: 44+

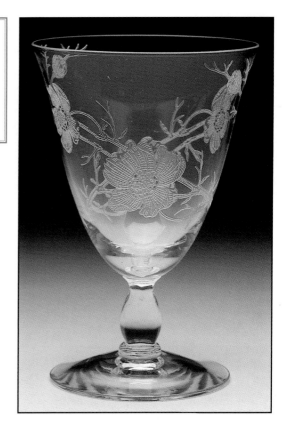

PATTERN NAME: MANDARIN, "GREEK
KEY," STEM #D-1
Company: Duncan & Miller
Years: c. 1940s
Colors: crystal
Items: 12

PATTERN NAME: MANHATTAN, #15078
Company: U.S. Glass Co.; Bartlett-Collins, Co.
Years: c. 1909; 1967
Colors: crystal, crystal with gold, red flash,
carnival; amber, crystal, moss green
Items: 32+

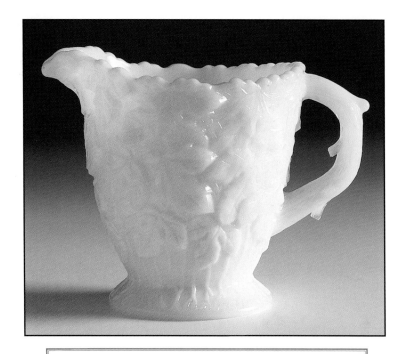

PATTERN NAME: MAPLE LEAF, "BRAMBLE,"
                  LINE #1928
Company: Westmoreland Glass Co.
Years: c. 1928
Colors: Milk glass, crystal
Items: 12

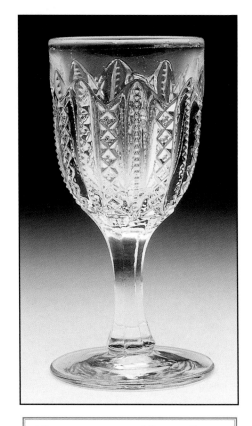

PATTERN NAME: MARDI GRAS
Company: Duncan & Miller
Years: c. 1940
Colors: crystal
Items: 3+

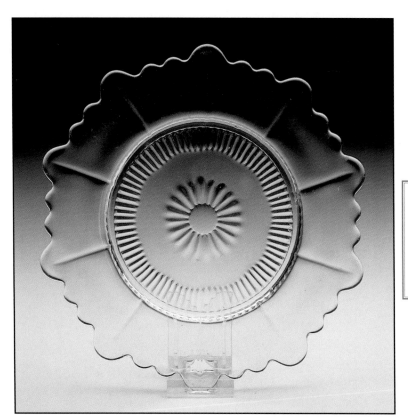

PATTERN NAME: MARTHA
Company: Cambridge Glass Co.
Years: 1930s
Colors: crystal
Items: 80+

PATTERN NAME: MARYLAND, #15049,
 "LOOP & FAN";
 "LOOP & DIAMOND"
Company: U.S. Glass Co.
Years: c. 1900
Colors: crystal, ruby stain
Items: 25

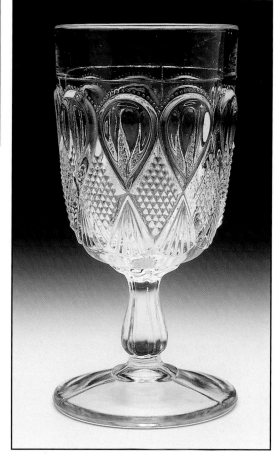

PATTERN NAME: MAYA #221
Company: Paden City Glass Mfg. Co.;
 Canton Glass Co.
Years: 1930s; 1950s
Colors: blue, crystal, ruby
Items: 12+

PATTERN NAME: MAYFAIR #2419
Company: Fostoria Glass Co.
Years: c. 1930s
Colors: amber, ebony, green, pink, ruby, topaz, wisteria
Items: 29+

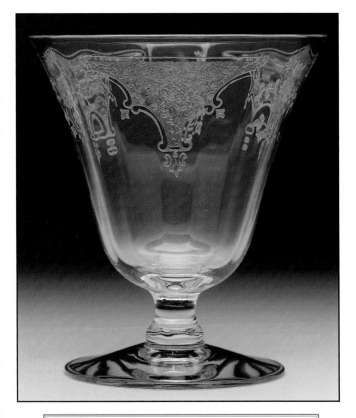

PATTERN NAME: "McGuire," Etch #1001, #4450 Blank
Company: Lotus Glass Company, Inc.
Years: c. 1930s
Colors: pink, black, crystal
Items: 17+
Note: Called Scroll, Etch 600; Seneca Glass Co. Stem Line

PATTERN NAME: Melrose, Etch #268
Company: Fostoria Glass Co.
Years: c. 1925
Colors: Crystal
Items: 50+

PATTERN NAME: MELROSE/GOLD
ENCRUST #633
Company: Tiffin Glass Co.
Years: 1930
Colors: crystal with gold
Items: 40

PATTERN NAME: MIKADO ETCH #808, #7711 CALLAHAN STEM
Company: Morgantown Glass Works
Colors: crystal
Items: 6

PATTERN NAME: MINERVA, #763 ETCH;
                                GADROON BLANK #3500
Company: Cambridge Glass Co.
Years: c. 1933
Colors: crystal; crystal with gold
Items: 30+

PATTERN NAME: MING
Company: Fenton Art Glass
Years: c. 1935
Colors: amber, Crystal, green, pink
                  with satin
Items: 60+

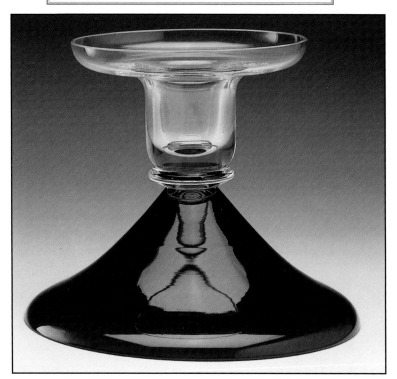

PATTERN NAME: MODERN, #6037
Company: Tiffin Glass Co.
Years: c. 1948
Colors: Kilarney Green, Crystal

PATTERN NAME: MODERN #17430
Company: Tiffin Glass Co.
Years: c. 1951
Colors: crystal, copen blue, wisteria
Items: 100+

PATTERN NAME: MODERNISTIC, "TRIAD"
                LINE #33
Company: New Martinsville Glass Mfg. Co.
Years: c. 1929
Colors: black; blue, green, pink, and
            with satin
Items: 13

PATTERN NAME: MONTICELLO,
                "WAFFLE BLOCK"
Company: Imperial Glass Co.
Years: c. 1930
Colors: Crystal, carnival, some
            pink, milk glass
Items: 35+

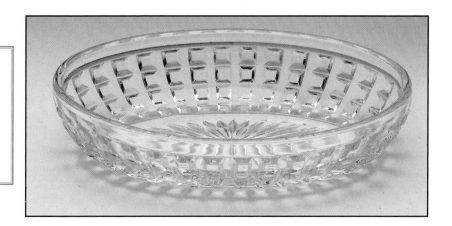

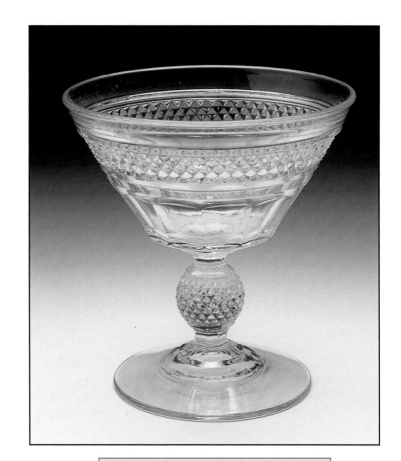

PATTERN NAME: MOONSTONE,
                          #2882
Company: Fostoria Glass Co.
Years: 1974
Colors: Apple green, blue, crystal,
               pink, taupe, yellow
Items: 6

PATTERN NAME: MT. VERNON
Company: Viking Glass Co.
Years: c. 1962
Colors: Red, yellow, cobalt
Items: 11

PATTERN NAME: MT. VERNON
                          #6991
Company: Imperial Glass Co.
Years: 1920s
Colors: crystal
Items: 35+

PATTERN NAME: MYRIAD, LINE #2592
Company: Fostoria Glass Co.
Years: 1941; 1950s
Colors: crystal, crystal with ebony,
ebony with gold
Items: 19

PATTERN NAME: MT. VERNON,
CUT #817;
BLANK #6031
Company: Fostoria Glass Co.
Years: c. 1942
Colors: crystal
Items: 17

PATTERN NAME: MYSTIC, ETCH #270
(PLAIN), #270½
(OPTIC)
Company: Fostoria Glass Co.
Years: c. 1925
Colors: crystal (plain), green
(spiral optic)
Items: 32

PATTERN NAME: "NARCISSUS
             SPRAY,"
             "BOUQUET"
Company: Indiana Glass Co.
Years: c. 1918
Colors: crystal, crystal with
          decorations
Items: 20+

PATTERN NAME: NATIONAL, SCROLL, S PATTERN,
             "S REPEAT," "REVERSE S,"
             "DANCING S" (ORIGINALLY ERIE)
Company: Dugan Glass Co.; Imperial Glass Co.;
         L.G. Wright Glass Co.
Years: 1903; 1970s
Colors: green, amber, red, blue, some amethyst,
         crystal
Items: 17+

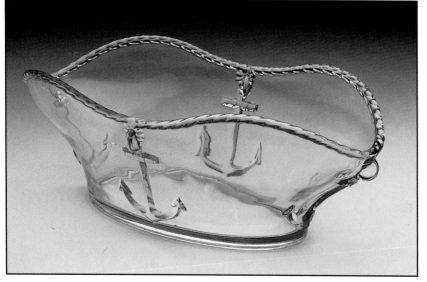

PATTERN NAME: NAUTICAL
Company: Duncan & Miller
Colors: Crystal; blue, opal blue,
         opal pink
Items: 30+

PATTERN NAME: NAVARRE,
　　　　　　　　CROWN
　　　　　　　　LINE, #2751
Company: Fostoria Glass Co.
Years: c. 1961
Colors: Crystal, Royal
　　　　　Blue, Gold, Ruby
Items: 4

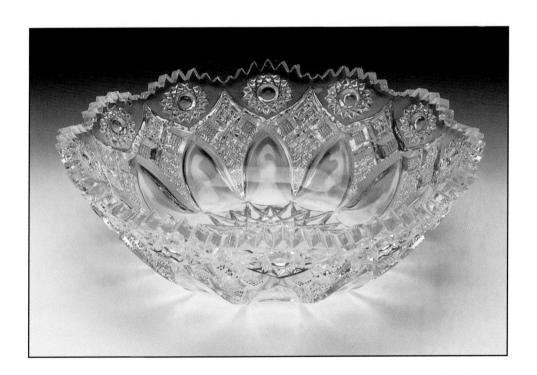

PATTERN NAME: NEARCUT #12 (12 ROSETTES, DARTS, ARCHES)
Company: H. Northwood & Co.
Years: c. 1906
Colors: crystal
Items: 34

PATTERN NAME: NEEDLE ETCH #365;
                STEM BLANK #325
Company: Bryce, Higbee & Co.
Years: c. 1916
Colors: crystal

PATTERN NAME: NOBILITY DESIGN, CUT
              #775; DOVER STEM #5330
Company: Duncan & Miller
Colors: Crystal

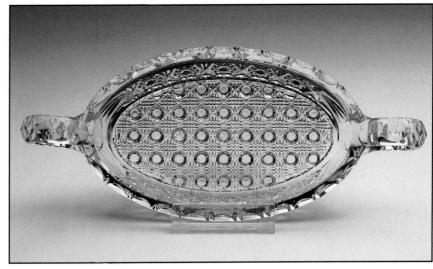

PATTERN NAME: NOSEGAY, CUT #824;
          BLANK #6051½
Company: Fostoria Glass Co.
Years: 1953
Colors: Crystal
Items: 25

PATTERN NAME: NUCUT, LINE #495
Company: Imperial Glass Co.
Years: c. 1937
Colors: crystal
Items: 1

PATTERN NAME: OCTAGON #1211
Company: Westmoreland Glass Co.
Years: 1930s
Colors: crystal, green, pink,
          various trims
Items: 45+

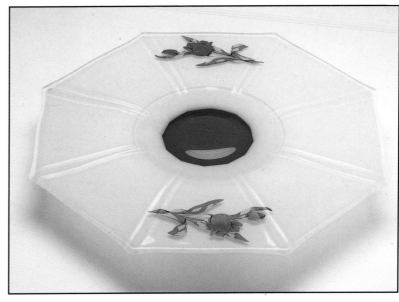

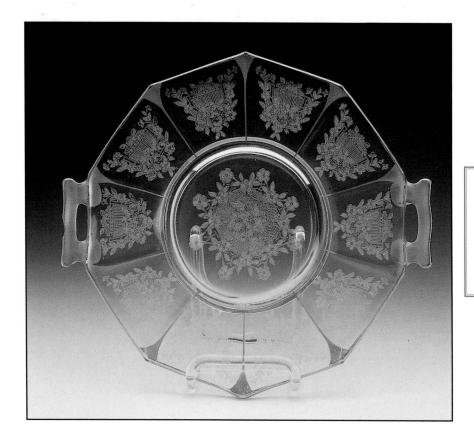

PATTERN NAME: OCTAGON #725
Company: Imperial Glass Co.
Years: c. 1930s
Colors: crystal, crystal with gold,
               opalescent blue, red
Items: 6+

PATTERN NAME: OLD DOMINION #3380
Company: A.H. Heisey & Co.
Years: c. 1925
Colors: Crystal with green; Sahara,
              Flamingo
Items: 22

PATTERN NAME: OLDE VIRGINIA
Company: Fenton Art Glass
Years: c. 1970
Colors: amber, cameo, colonial colors,
milk glass, ruby, opalescent
Items: 16

PATTERN NAME: "ORANGE PEEL," LINE #69
Company: Westmoreland Glass Co.
Years: 1910
Colors: Orange with crystal
Items: 4

PATTERN NAME: ORIENTAL, ETCH
#250; BLANK #766
Company: Fostoria Glass Co.
Years: 1918
Colors: Crystal
Items: 70+

PATTERN NAME: PANEL GRAPE
Company: L.G. Wright Glass Co.
Years: 1930s
Colors: blue, crystal, green, amethyst, ruby, yellow
Items: 24+

PATTERN NAME: PALM OPTIC,
            VENUS STEM #7577
Company: Morgantown Glass Works
Years: 1918
Colors: Anna Rose, crystal, blue,
            topaz, green, aquamarine,
            crystal with ebony,
            bi-color
Items: 6

PATTERN NAME: PANELED HEATHER
Years: c. 1890s
Colors: Crystal, crystal with gold
Items: 16+

PATTERN NAME: "PANELED SMOCKING,"
            LINE #65
Company: Bartlett-Collins;
          Tiffin Glass Co.
Colors: Crystal, red, marigold
Items: 3

PATTERN NAME: PANSY BASKET WITH SPLIT HANDLE, LINE #757
Company: Westmoreland Glass Co.
Years: c. 1970s
Colors: crystal with ruby stain, blue, mint, milk glass, crystal,
           flame, green and purple marble, mist, antique blue
Items: 1

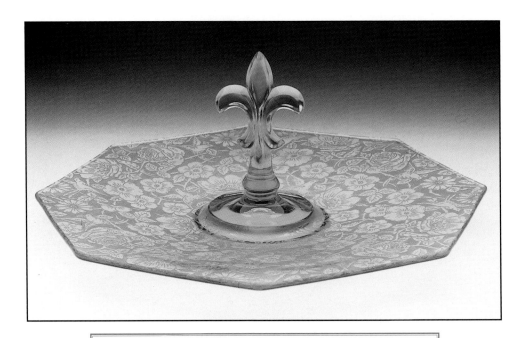

PATTERN NAME: PARADISE, BROCADE ETCH #289,
BLANK #2342
Company: Fostoria Glass Co.
Years: 1927
Colors: green, orchid
Items: 19

PATTERN NAME: PARKWOOD ENGRAVING
Company: Tiffin Glass Co.
Years: c. 1942
Colors: crystal; crystal with ruby stain

PATTERN NAME: PATTERN #308;
             BLANK #10
Company: Various companies'
          wares for Ft. Dearborn
          Sales Catalogue; New
          Martinsville Glass Co.
Years: c. 1930
Colors: cased green and blue
Items: 20

PATTERN NAME: PAULINA
Company: Tiffin Glass Co.
Years: c. 1930s
Colors: mandarin, rose, topaz
Items: 50

PATTERN NAME: PAVONIA; PINEAPPLE STEM
Company: Ripley & Co.; U.S. Glass Co.
Years: c. mid-1880s; 1890s
Colors: Crystal, crystal with ruby stain
Items: 18

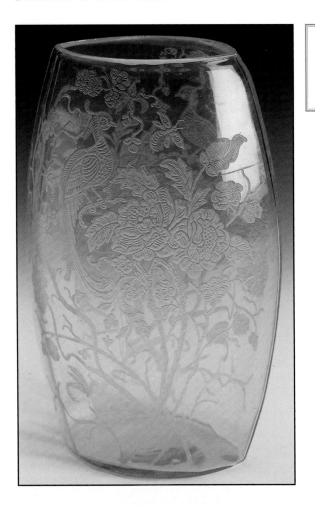

PATTERN NAME: PEACOCK & WILD ROSE
Company: Paden City Glass Mfg. Co.
Colors: pink, green, black, cobalt,
            amber, crystal, light blue

PATTERN NAME: PEBBLE BEACH #2806
Company: Fostoria Glass Co.
Years: 1969
Colors: Crystal, Blue, yellow, pink,
            orange, black pearl
Items: 17

PATTERN NAME: PERSIAN #702
Company: Morgantown Glass Works

PATTERN NAME: "PETAL" DECORATION,
#1800 PLAIN LINE
Company: Westmoreland Glass Co.
Years: c. 1928
Colors: applied blue, green
Items: 4+

PATTERN NAME: "PETAL LANDRUM" #767/7
Company: Lancaster Glass Co.
Years: 1932
Colors: topaz, rose
Items: 4

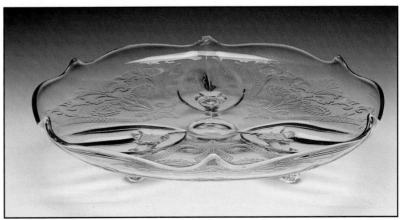

PATTERN NAME: PETITE,
            STEM #17595
Company: Tiffin Glass Co.

PATTERN NAME: PICARDY ETCH; #7646
            SOPHISTICATE STEM
Company: Morgantown Glass Works
Years: c. 1931
Colors: crystal
Items: 8

PATTERN NAME: PILAR FLUTE #682
Company: Imperial Glass Co.
Years: c. 1920s, off/on through 1970s
Colors: Iridescent red glow, Iridescent blue glow, crystal, marigold, smoke, clambroth
Items: 30+

PATTERN NAME: PILLOW ENCIRCLED, MIDWAY #857
Company: Model Flint Glass Works
Years: c. 1890
Colors: crystal, crystal with ruby flash
Items: 19

PATTERN NAME: PINE, CUT #835;
                        CONTOUR BLANK #2666
Company: Fostoria Glass Co.
Years: c. 1950s
Colors: Crystal
Items: 30+

PATTERN NAME: "PINEAPPLE"
Company: Indiana Glass Co.
Years: c. 1980s
Colors: crystal, milk glass, yellow,
           blue
Items: 1

PATTERN NAME: PINEAPPLE & FAN
Company: A. H. Heisey & Co.
Years: c. 1897
Colors: emerald green with gold,
           crystal with gold
Items: 70+

PATTERN NAME: "PINWHEEL,"
          "STAR FLOWER"
Company: U.S. Glass Co.
Years: c. 1925
Colors: green
Items: 6+

PATTERN NAME: "PLAID," #124, "BERLIN"
Company: Westmoreland Glass Co.
Years: 1924; 1980s
Colors: crystal, green, pink; ruby
Items: 16

PATTERN NAME: PLAINWARE #1917/4
Company: Cambridge Glass Co.
Years: c. 1922
Colors: Azurite, crystal, ebony
Items: 65+

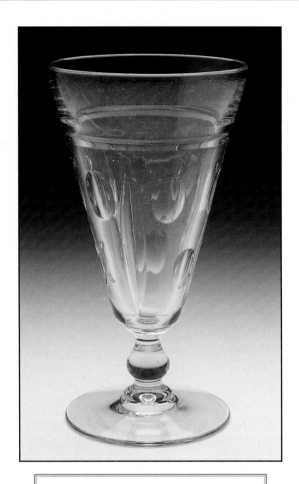

PATTERN NAME: PLANET
Company: Model Flint Glass Co.
Years: 1899
Colors: Crystal
Items: 15

PATTERN NAME: PLAZA, NO. 21
Company: Duncan & Miller
Colors: crystal, pink, ruby
Items: 28

PATTERN NAME: "PLEAT RIBS" #2425
Company: Fostoria Glass Co.
Years: 1928
Colors: rose, azure, amber, crystal, ebony, topaz

PATTERN NAME: POGO STICK,
CROWN
Company: Lancaster Glass Co.
Years: c. 1910

PATTERN NAME: POMPEII, #449
Company: A.H. Heisey & Co.
Years: 1931
Colors: crystal, Sahara
Items: 28

PATTERN NAME: "POPEYE & OLIVE," LINE #994
Company: Paden City Glass Mfg. Co.
Years: c. 1932
Colors: ruby, cobalt
Items: 14

PATTERN NAME: POPPY, #14196
Company: Tiffin Glass Co.
Years: c. 1925
Colors: crystal, vases in satin blue
Items: 19+

PATTERN NAME: PRESCUT #836
Company: Anchor Hocking Glass Corp.
Years: c. 1940s
Colors: crystal
Items: 1

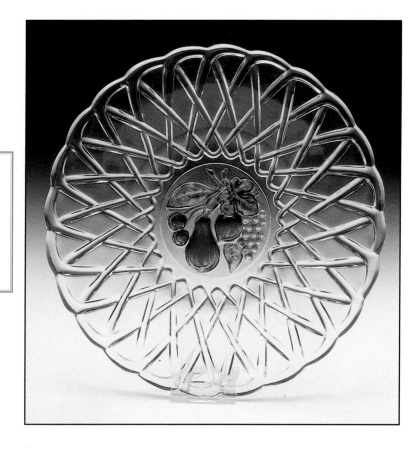

PATTERN NAME: PRETZEL WITH
                INTAGLIO, #622
Company: Indiana Glass Co.
Years: c. 1930s
Colors: crystal, teal, amber, crystal
          with trim, blue, avocado
Items: 4

PATTERN NAME: PRINCESS FEATHER,
                LINE #201
Company: Westmoreland Glass Co.
Years: 1924
Colors: pink, blue, aqua, green,
          crystal, amber
Items: 25+

PATTERN NAME: PRINCESS (GOLD ENCRUSTED ETCH);
                MEMOIR STEM #17680
Company: Tiffin Glass Co.
Years: c. 1930
Colors: crystal with gold

PATTERN NAME: PRINCESS, LINE #5222
Company: Viking Glass Co.
Years: 1952
Colors: crystal

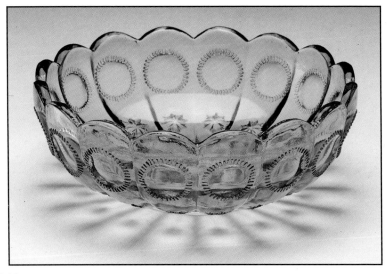

PATTERN NAME: PRISCILLA; MOON AND
                STAR; ALEXIS
Company: Dalzell, Gilmore & Leighton;
           Fenton Art Glass;
           L.G. Wright Glass Co.
Years: 1890s; 1950s; 1960s
Colors: crystal; amber, green, red
Items: 23+

PATTERN NAME: PRISM BAND, #1014
Company: Fenton Art Glass
Years: c. 1912
Colors: Royal Blue
Items: 2

PATTERN NAME: PRISMATIC LINE, #979 "SWIRL RIB"
Company: Anchor Hocking Glass Corp.
Years: c. 1941
Colors: crystal, pink
Items: 2

PATTERN NAME: PUNTY BAND, #1220
Company: A. H. Heisey & Co.
Years: c. 1896
Colors: crystal, custard, opal,
          ruby flash
Items: 60+

PATTERN NAME: PUNTY & DIAMOND POINT, #305
Company: A.H. Heisey & Co.
Years: c. 1898
Colors: crystal
Items: 21+

PATTERN NAME: PURITAN
Company: McKee; Jeanette Glass Works;
          Fenton Art Glass
Years: 1890s; 1904; 1990s
Colors: crystal; salem blue; black carnival
Items: 69

PATTERN NAME: PURITAN (BLANK),
                         ETCH UNIDENTIFIED
Company: Duncan & Miller
Years: c. 1929
Colors: crystal, green, rose
Items: 13+

PATTERN NAME: PURITAN
                         DECORATION #8105
Company: U.S. Glass Co.
Years: 1926
Colors: pink satin
Items: 12

PATTERN NAME: QUEEN ANN, #365
Company: A.H. Heisey & Co.
Years: c. 1906
Colors: crystal
Items: 50+

PATTERN NAME: "RADIAL LINE" DECORATION, #1800 PLAIN LINE
Company: Westmoreland Glass Co.
Years: 1913
Colors: crystal, opal; 1930s colors
Items: 4+

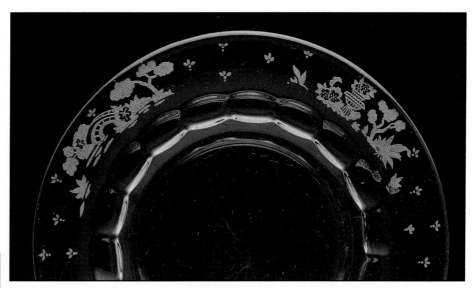

PATTERN NAME: RALEIGH (BLANK #2574) WITH WILLOW
ETCH #335
Company: Fostoria Glass Co.
Years: 1939
Colors: crystal
Items: 33

PATTERN NAME: RALEIGH, ETCH
#162; BILTMORE
BLANK #3316
Company: A. H. Heisey & Co.
Years: 1918
Colors: crystal
Items: 7

PATTERN NAME: "RAM'S HEAD," GADROON LINE #3350
WITH "ELAINE" ETCH
Company: Cambridge Glass Co.; Imperial Glass Co.
Years: c. 1930s; 1970
Colors: crystal, blue, crown tuscan; cobalt iridescent,
jade, ebony, rubina, ivory with ram
Items: 4+

PATTERN NAME: RAMBLER, ETCH #323;
                      BLANK #6012
Company: Fostoria Glass Co.
Years: c. 1935
Colors: crystal
Items: 50+

PATTERN NAME: RAMBLER ROSE,
                      LINE #196 WIDE OPTIC
Company: Tiffin Glass Co.
Years: 1931
Colors: crystal, rose
Items: 40

PATTERN NAME: RAY, "SWIRL AND BALL"
Company: McKee & Brothers
Years: c. 1894
Colors: crystal

PATTERN NAME: REFLECTION (NEW SHEFFIELD)
Company: Fenton Art Glass
Years: 1986
Colors: Minted Creme, Peaches 'n Cream, Velva Rose (Blue)
Items: 3

PATTERN NAME: REGENCY PETALWARE #28920
Company: Macbeth-Evans Division Corning Glass Works
Years: c. 1939
Colors: Ivorian, B374 gold
Items: 6

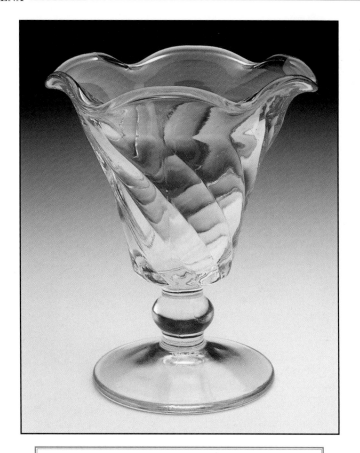

PATTERN NAME: RENA, LINE #154
Company: Paden City Glass Mfg. Co.
Years: c. 1930
Colors: crystal, green, pink
Items: 42

PATTERN NAME: REYER THISTLE,
              ETCH; GALAXY STEM
              #7668
Company: Morgantown Glass Works
Colors: Crystal
Items: 9

PATTERN NAME: "RIB OVER DRAPE"
Company: U.S. Glass Co.
Colors: crystal
Items: 4

PATTERN NAME: RICHLIEU
Company: Seneca Glass Co.

PATTERN NAME: RICHMOND, ETCH #735;
#7589 LAURETTE STEM
Company: Morgantown Glass Works
Years: c. 1918
Colors: crystal
Items: 5

PATTERN NAME: "RING & PETAL," NO. 1875
Company: Westmoreland Glass Co.
Years: c. 1970s
Colors: milk glass, yellow mist, coraline, blue
Items: 10

PATTERN NAME: RINGMONT #99181
Company: Bryce, Higbee & Co.

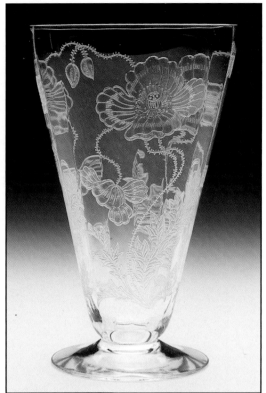

PATTERN NAME: ROCOCO
Company: Imperial Glass Co.
Years: 1910
Colors: marigold; smoke
Items: 3

PATTERN NAME: ROGENE, ETCH
#269, BLANK #4095
Company: Fostoria Glass Co.
Years: c. 1925
Colors: crystal
Items: 60+

PATTERN NAME: ROMAN ROSETTE
Company: U.S. Glass Co.
Years: c. 1891, reproduction goblet
1945
Colors: crystal, crystal with ruby
stain
Items: 20+

PATTERN NAME: ROSALIND
Company: Tiffin Glass Co.
Years: 1932
Colors: Crystal, mandarin
Items: 50+

PATTERN NAME: ROSE DESIGN #827,
                CONTOUR BLANK
                #2666
Company: Fostoria Glass Co.
Years: c. 1951
Items: 38

PATTERN NAME: ROSE POINT BAND,
              "WATERLILY,"
              "CLEMATIS"
Company: Indiana Glass Co.
Years: c. 1915
Colors: crystal
Items: 11

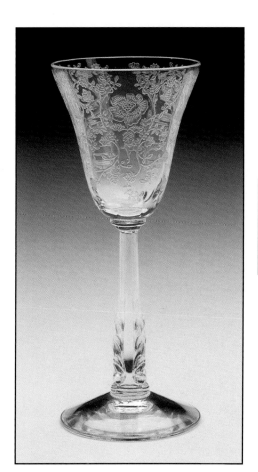

PATTERN NAME: ROSEPOINT
Company: Imperial Glass Co.
Years: c. 1950s
Colors: Crystal with gold

PATTERN NAME: ROSELYN #3779
Company: Cambridge Glass Co.
Years: c. 1950
Colors: crystal

PATTERN NAME: ROSES, DEEP ETCH #18;
                    BLANK #7715
Company: H.C. Fry Glass Co.
Years: c. 1914
Colors: crystal
Items: 21

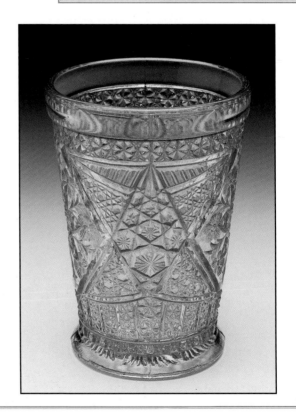

PATTERN NAME: ROSETTE WITH PINWHEELS #171
Company: Indiana Glass Co.
Years: c. 1932
Colors: crystal
Items: 13

PATTERN NAME: ROTEC (PRESCUT
STAMP)
Company: McKee; John E. Kemple
Glass Works
Years: 1904; 1960s
Colors: Crystal; various colors
and milk glass
Items: 42+

PATTERN NAME: "SATINTONE,"
AMERICAN WAY
BLANK, #714
Company: Duncan & Miller
Colors: crystal
Items: 24

PATTERN NAME: "SATURN RINGS,"
LINE #2362
Company: Fostoria Glass Co.
Years: c. 1926
Colors: amber, blue, green,
orchid

PATTERN NAME: "SCOTTIES"
Company: H.C. Fry Company
Years: c. 1930

PATTERN NAME: "SCROLL AND PLUME," ETCH #711; BLANK #428
Company: Cambridge Glass Co.
Years: c. 1920s
Colors: Green, crystal
Items: 6

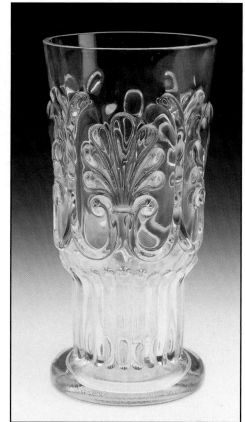

PATTERN NAME: SCROLL, ATTERBURY SCROLL
Company: Imperial Glass Co.
Years: 1960s; early 1980s
Colors: crystal, jade, milk glass
Items: 27

PATTERN NAME: SCROLL, ETCH #600
Company: Seneca Glass Co.
Colors: amber, crystal

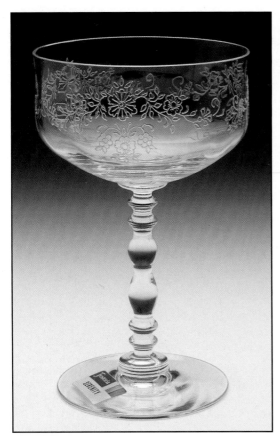

PATTERN NAME: SERENITY, ETCH #35
Company: Fostoria Glass Co.
Years: c. 1975
Colors: blue and yellow with crystal; crystal
Items: 5

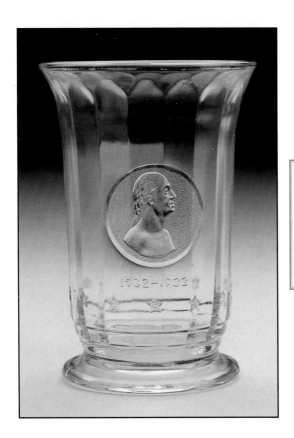

PATTERN NAME: SESQUICENTENNIAL GLASS,
                WASHINGTON #1892
Company: Hazel Atlas Glass Co.
Years: c. 1932
Colors: Topaz, green, crystal
Items: 1

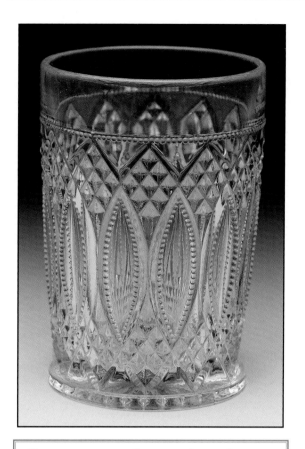

PATTERN NAME: SHARPE OVAL &
DIAMOND BAND,
LOUISIANA
#15053
Company: U.S. Glass Co. (Bryce Plant)
Years: c. 1898
Colors: crystal
Items: 23

PATTERN NAME: SHELL AND CLUB, NO. 30
Company: John E. Kemple Glass Works
Years: c. 1940s
Colors: milk glass
Items: 2

PATTERN NAME: SHEPHERD'S PLAID
Company: Model Flint Glass Co.
Years: 1896
Colors: crystal, green
Items: 15+

PATTERN NAME: SHERATON, LINE #550
Company: Bartlett-Collins
Years: late 1920s
Colors: Nu-green, Nu-rose
Items: 11

PATTERN NAME: SILVERDALE #17492
PLATINUM BAND
Company: Tiffin Glass Co.

PATTERN NAME: "SIX PETAL" #1413
Company: Viking Glass Co.
Years: 1970s
Colors: Amethyst
Items: 1

PATTERN NAME: "SNAIL
SCROLL,"
BLANK #2536
CORSAGE,
ETCH #325
Company: Fostoria Glass Co.
Years: c. 1936
Colors: crystal
Items: 2

PATTERN NAME: "SODA FOUNTAIN LINE,"
"PARTY LINE" #191 & 191½
Company: Paden City Glass Mfg. Co.
Years: 1930
Colors: amber, green, pink, crystal
Items: 35+ (soda items); 100+ (dinnerware)

PATTERN NAME: SORENO
Company: Anchor Hocking
Glass Corp
Years: 1966
Colors: aqua, avocado,
white, crystal,
honey, aurora,
lustre, mardi
gras
Items: 33+

PATTERN NAME: SORRENTO, #2832
Company: Fostoria Glass Co.
Years: c. 1974
Colors: Blue, Green, Brown, Plum, Pink
Items: 7

PATTERN NAME: SPARTAN ETCH/
PLATINUM #769
Company: Morgantown Glass Works
Years: c. 1930
Colors: Ritz blue
Items: 2+

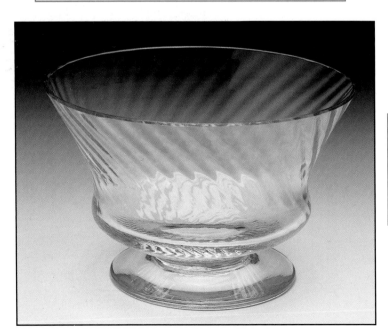

PATTERN NAME: SPIRAL OPTIC, LINE #022
Company: Tiffin Glass Co.
Years: c. 1923
Colors: crystal with green, green, pink
Items: 14

PATTERN NAME: SPLENDOR, NO. 6131
Company: Fostoria Glass Co.
Years: c. 1978
Colors: Blue, rust
Items: 4

PATTERN NAME: SPORTSMAN #455 ETCH;
            GASCONY #3397 BLANK
Company: A.H. Heisey & Co.
Years: c. 1932
Colors: crystal
Items: 36

PATTERN NAME: SPRAY, CUT #841;
            STEM BLANK #6055½
Company: Fostoria Glass Co.
Years: c. 1950s
Colors: crystal
Items: 24

PATTERN NAME: SPRING BEAUTY,
                BLANK #D5
Company: Duncan & Miller

PATTERN NAME: "SPRING BOW,"
                NEEDLE ETCH #305;
                #13630 BLANK
Company: Tiffin Glass Co.
Years: 1924
Colors: crystal
Items: 16

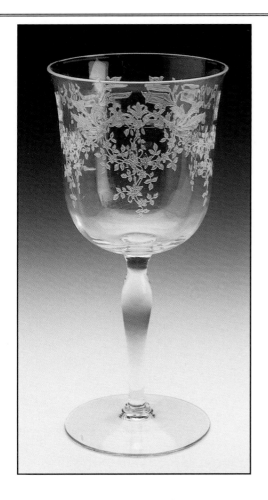

PATTERN NAME: SPRINGTIME, ETCH #318;
                     BLANK #891
Company: Fostoria Glass Co.
Years: c. 1930s
Colors: Crystal, Topaz
Items: 90+

PATTERN NAME: SPRITE, CUT #823;
                     MADEMOISELLE BLANK #6033
Company: Fostoria Glass Co.
Years: 1950
Colors: Crystal
Items: 30+

PATTERN NAME: "STAGECOACH"
Company: H.C. Fry Glass Co.
Years: c. 1930

PATTERN NAME: "STANDARD," #1648
Company: Standard Glass Mfg. Co.
Years: c. 1926
Colors: pink
Items: 2

PATTERN NAME: STAR BAND;
         "BOSWORTH"
Company: Indiana Glass Co.
Years: c. 1907
Colors: crystal; crystal with
       ruby, crystal with gold

PATTERN NAME: "STAR MEDALLION," "STAR & FILE," LINE #612
Company: Imperial Glass Co.
Years: c. 1920s
Colors: marigold, smoke, green, purple carnival, crystal,
aurora, milk glass
Items: 20+

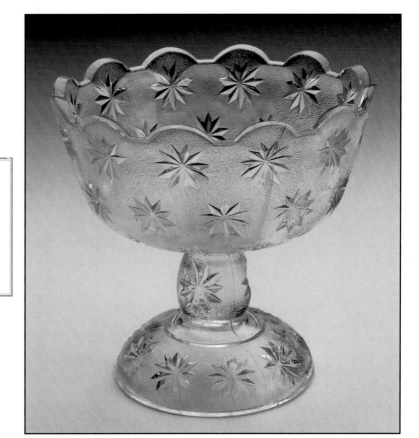

PATTERN NAME: STAR; STIPPLED
SANDBURR
Company: Beatty-Brady Glass Co.;
Westmoreland Glass Co.
Years: c. 1903; 1915
Colors: crystal
Items: 8+

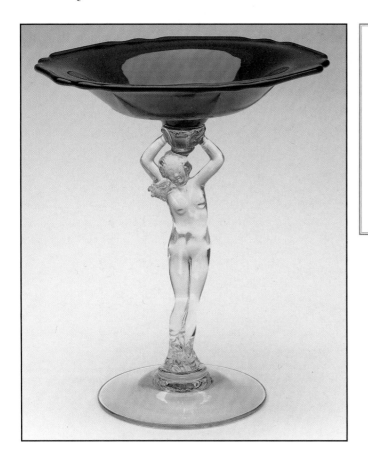

PATTERN NAME: STATUESQUE, LINE #3011
Company: Cambridge Glass Co.
Years: c. 1931
Colors: bi colors of amber, crystal, Gold Krystol, Heatherbloom, Amethyst, Carmen, Emerald (dark) green, Forest Green, LaRosa, Mandarin Gold, Mocha, Moonlight, Pistachio, Pink, Royal Blue, Smoke, Tahoe Blue, Topaz, Ebony – both with and without optic
Items: 20+

PATTERN NAME: STEM #033 (15033); PERSIAN PHEASANT ETCH
Company: Tiffin Glass Co.
Years: c. 1930
Colors: crystal, rose
Items: 14+

PATTERN NAME: STRADIVARI; REGENCY
(8 COLOR HARLEQUIN
SETS, 1940S)
Company: Cambridge Glass Co.
Years: c. 1937 – 41; 1949 – 50s
Colors: Tahoe Blue, Moonlight blue,
Forest Green, Gold Krystol,
La Rosa, Mocha, Amethyst,
Pistachio, crystal with etchings,
crystal
Items: 11

PATTERN NAME: "STURDY" LINE #557
Company: Cooperative Flint Glass Co.
Years: c. 1930s
Colors: crystal, green, amber, pink,
cobalt, topaz, ruby, black
Items: 20

PATTERN NAME: SUNBURST #018 CORONA LINE
Company: Tiffin Glass Co.

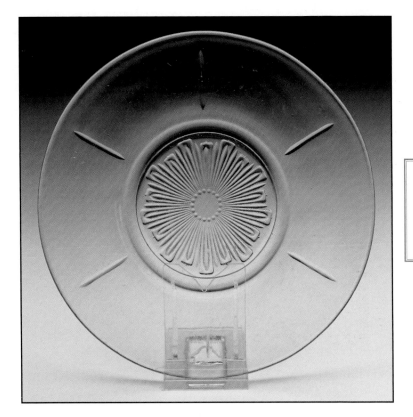

PATTERN NAME: "SUNFLOWER"
Company: U.S. Glass Co.
Years: c. 1925
Colors: green
Items: 6+

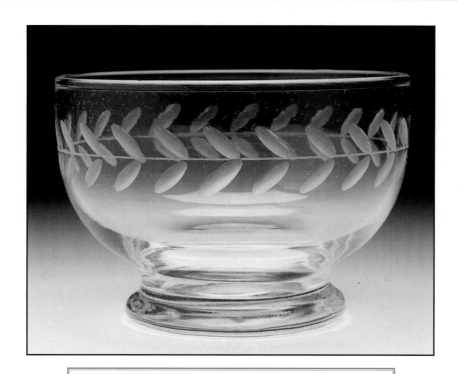

PATTERN NAME: SWEDISH MODERN, CUT 411
Company: Anchor Hocking Corp.
Years: c. 1959
Colors: crystal
Items: 16

PATTERN NAME: SWIRL, LINE #1001
Company: Duncan & Miller
Colors: Sapphire, green, pink, amber, crystal

PATTERN NAME: "SWIRLING HEARTS
OR SPADES"
Company: Hobbs Glass Works;
U.S. Glass Co.
Years: c. 1890s
Colors: crystal; crystal with
amber or ruby
Items: 4

PATTERN NAME: TEA ROSE,
ETCH #504;
TRIDENT #134
BLANK
Company: A.H. Heisey & Co.
Years: 1940
Colors: crystal

PATTERN NAME: TEARDROP, #1011
Company: Indiana Glass Co.
Years: 1950s
Colors: milk glass, crystal with
stains (ruby, green, plum)
Items: 15+

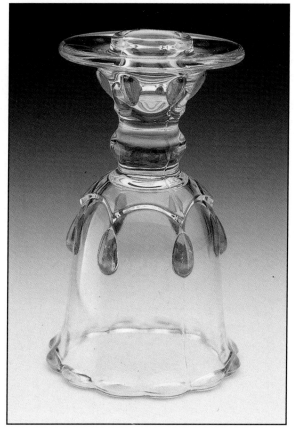

PATTERN NAME: TEN RIB OPTIC
Company: Tiffin Glass Co.
Years: c. 1950s
Colors: Kilarney Green, crystal,
          iridescent, Wisteria,
          cobalt, Twilight & Smoke,
          crystal & ruby, plum

PATTERN NAME: THISTLE #14180
Company: Tiffin Glass Co.
Years: 1929
Colors: crystal
Items: 20+

PATTERN NAME: "THISTLE" NO. 10 OPTIC;
              SPECIAL THISTLE, #14197
Company: Central Glass Works;
          Tiffin Glass Co.
Years: c. 1909; 1924
Colors: Crystal
Items: 36; 12

PATTERN NAME: THREE FACES #400; THREE FACES,
　　　　　　　LINE #65
Company: George Duncan & Sons; Duncan & Miller;
　　　　　　L.G. Wright Glass Co.; A.A. Importing Co.,
　　　　　　Inc; Imperial Glass Co.
Years:　　　1880s; 1950s; late 1960s;
　　　　　　last two, mid-1970s
Colors:　　 Crystal, and with satin
Items:　　　20+ (old); up to 14 (new)

PATTERN NAME: TIFFIN ROSE,
　　　　　　　later RAMBLING
　　　　　　　ROSE/PEARL
　　　　　　　EDGE BLANK
Company: Tiffin Glass Co.
Years:　　 c. 1948
Colors:　　Crystal
Items:　　 80

PATTERN NAME: TOP PRIZE
Company: New Martinsville
          Glass Mfg. Co.
Colors: Crystal, red
Items: 6+

PATTERN NAME: TOURRAINE, #337
Company: A.H. Heisey & Co.
Years: c. 1902
Colors: Amber, crystal
Items: 70+

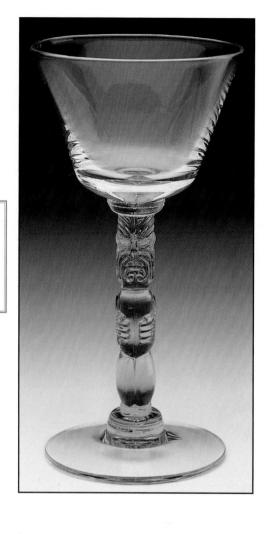

PATTERN NAME: TRADER VIC/MAI TAI
Company: Imperial Glass Co./Morgantown
Years: c. 1960
Colors: Amber, Topaz with crystal
Items: 3

PATTERN NAME: TRANSITION,
              BLANK #2936
Company: Fostoria Glass Co.
Years: c. 1978
Colors: crystal
Items: 7

PATTERN NAME: TRELLIS, CUT #822;
             OPTIC STEM #6030
Company: Fostoria Glass Co.
Years: c. 1950
Colors: crystal
Items: 12

PATTERN NAME: "TRELLIS FLOWER,"
            DESIGN #229
Company: Westmoreland Speciality Co.
Years: c. 1925
Colors: crystal with amber stain

PATTERN NAME: TROJAN #6712
Company: U.S. Glass Co.
Years: 1926
Colors: crystal, green
Items: 13

PATTERN NAME: TRIUMPH, BLANK #6112
Company: Fostoria Glass Co.
Years: 1968
Colors: Silver and Gold Metal with Crystal
Items: 4

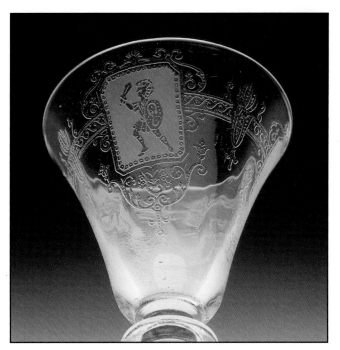 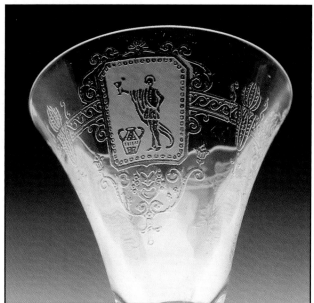

PATTERN NAME: TROJAN, ETCH #445; STEM #366
Company: A.H. Heisey & Co.
Years: 1928
Colors: crystal, crystal with Moongleam, green satin, flamingo
Items: 13

PATTERN NAME: "TROPHY CUP VASE,"
                    LINE #473
Company: L.E. Smith Glass Co.
Years: c. 1930s
Colors: Black

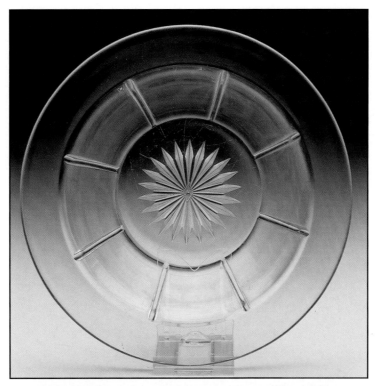

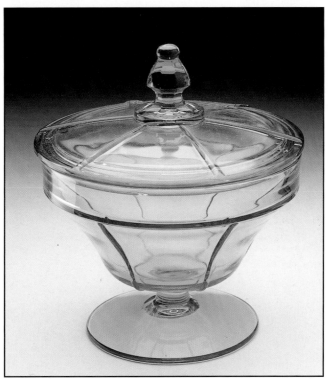

PATTERN NAME: TUDOR OR RIB & PANEL #411
Company: A.H. Hisey & Co.
Years: 1923
Colors: Moongleam, Flamingo, Hawthorne, crystal
Items: 62

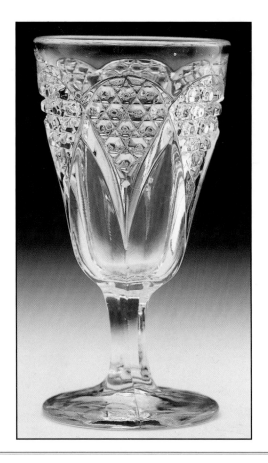

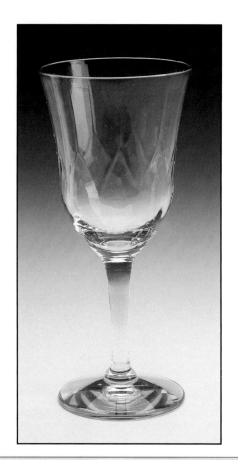

PATTERN NAME: TULIP & CANE, "KITE & PANEL" #9
Company: Imperial Glass Co.
Years: c. 1920s
Colors: Crystal, Carnival, Marigold, Smoke
Items: 5

PATTERN NAME: TULIP OPTIC, VENUS
BLANK #7577
Company: Morgantown Glass Works
Years: c. 1920s
Colors: Anna rose, aquamarine
Items: 6

PATTERN NAME: TWENTIETH CENTURY #1415
Company: A.H. Heisey & Co.
Years: c. 1931
Colors: Dawn, Moongleam, Flamingo
Items: 6

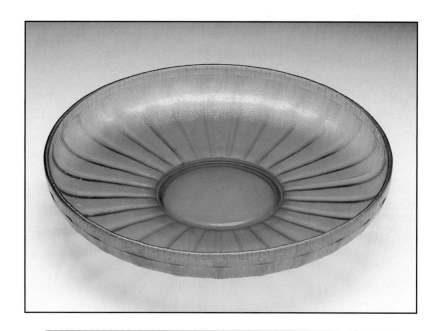

PATTERN NAME: TWENTY SEVEN RAYS, LINE #638
Company: Fenton Art Glass
Colors: Celeste Blue

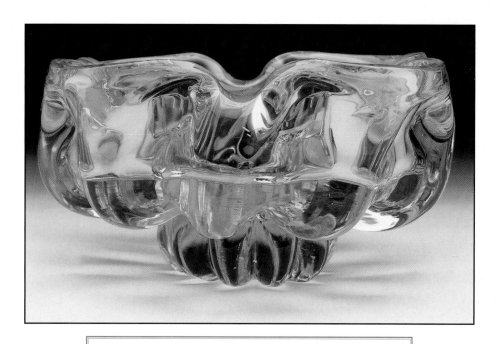

PATTERN NAME: "TWILIGHT," #1 (CIGAR TRAY)
Company: Tiffin Glass Co.
Years: c. 1950s
Colors: Twilight

PATTERN NAME: "TWIN DOLPHIN," #1621
Company: Fenton Art Glass
Years: c. 1936
Colors: Satintone Crystal, royal blue
Items: 10

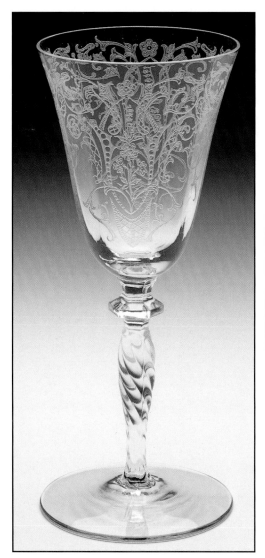

PATTERN NAME: "TWIST" STEM #117;
                        ETCH #606
Company: Tiffin Glass Co.
Years: c. 1930s
Colors: crystal, green
Items: 7

PATTERN NAME: U.S. COIN, "SILVER AGE";
"FROSTED COIN"
Company: U.S. Glass Co.; Central Glass Works;
A.A. Importing Co.
Years: c. 1890s; 1970s
Colors: Crystal, crystal with satin, crystal with
ruby or bronze stain; crystal with satin,
vaseline
Items: 30; 10

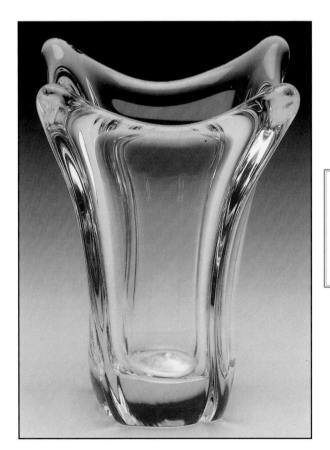

PATTERN NAME: VENETIAN, LINE #126
Company: Duncan & Miller
Years: c. 1932
Colors: crystal
Items: 12+

PATTERN NAME: VENUS, CUT #826;
                      #4044 NEW ERA BLANK
Company: A.H. Heisey & Co.
Years: 1936
Colors: Crystal

PATTERN NAME: VICTORIA, DAISY &
                      SCROLL, #15104
Company: U.S. Glass Co.
Years: early 1900s
Colors: Crystal with gold or green
Items: 8+

PATTERN NAME: VICTORIA, LINE #183
Company: Fostoria Glass Co.
Years: c. 1893
Colors: crystal
Items: 30+

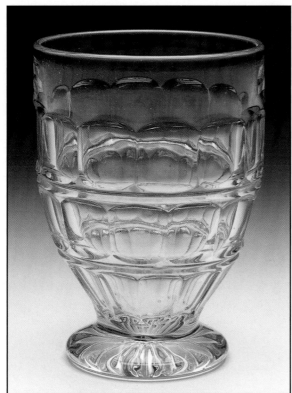

PATTERN NAME: VICTORIAN
Company: Duncan & Miller
Colors: Pink
Items: 19

PATTERN NAME: VICTORY, ETCH #257
Company: Fostoria Glass Co.
Years: 1922
Colors: crystal, crystal with gold,
            crystal with blue
Items: 64

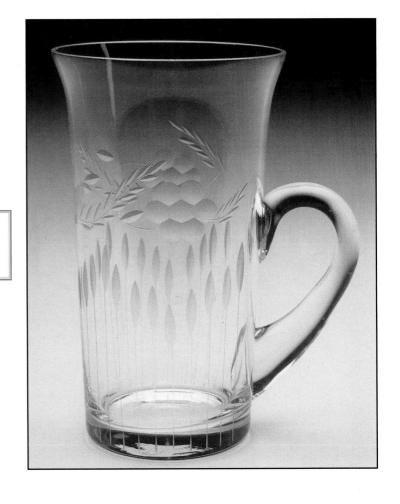

PATTERN NAME: VINE LINE #38
Company: Glastonbury Lotus

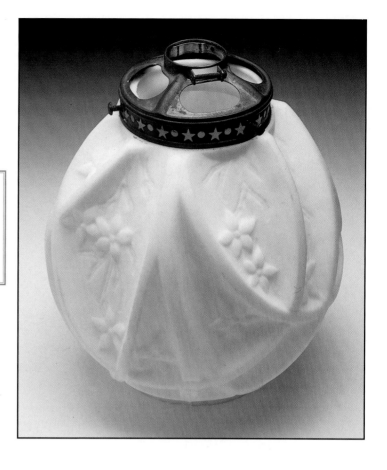

PATTERN NAME: VINE #700, MARTELE VINE
Company: Consolidated Lamp and Glass Co.
Years: c. 1926; 1937
Colors: Ruby on crystal, Gold on white
Items: 20

PATTERN NAME: VINTAGE, #473; NIAGARA GRAPE
Company: Imperial Glass Co.
Years: c. 1915
Colors: Clambroth, marigold, smoke
Items: 23

PATTERN NAME: VINTAGE GRAPE #9921
Company: L.E. Smith Glass Co.
Years: 1963

PATTERN NAME: WAFFLE
Company: Jeannette Glass Co.
Years: c. 1939
Colors: crystal
Items: 8

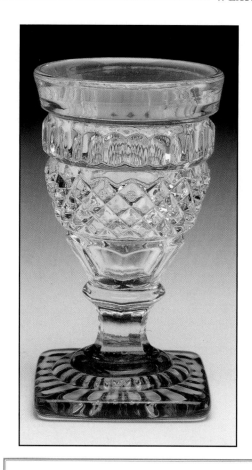

PATTERN NAME: WATERCRESS, CUT #741;
                          WESTCHESTER #6012-STEM
Company: Fostoria Glass Co.
Years: 1930s
Colors: Crystal
Items: 15

PATTERN NAME: WATERFORD #300
Company: Westmoreland Glass Co.
Year: c.1927
Colors: crystal with ruby and gold
Items: 41

PATTERN NAME: WEATHERFORD
Company: Cambridge Glass Co.
Years: c. 1926
Colors: amber, green, pink
Items: 25

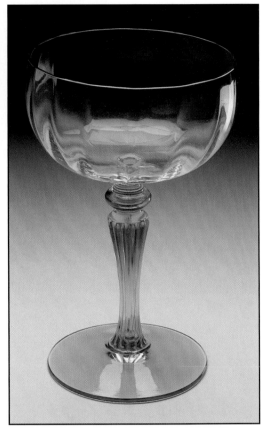

PATTERN NAME: WEDDING BELLS, #789
Company: Fostoria Glass Co.
Years: c. 1901
Colors: crystal, crystal with gold
Items: 25

PATTERN NAME: WIDE OPTIC, #016
Company: Tiffin Glass Co.
Colors: crystal with green trim
Items: 15

PATTERN NAME: WIDE OPTIC #354
Company: Tiffin Glass Co.
Years: 1922
Colors: Pink

PATTERN NAME: WILD GOOSE
Company: The Phoenix
                 Glass Co.
Years: c. 1940s
Colors: milk glass, crystal,
                 cameo, green, yellow,
                 red, tan, slate,
                 brown

PATTERN NAME: WILD ROSE ETCH #30; BLANK #42
Company: New Martinsville Glass Co.

PATTERN NAME: WILLIAMSBURG
(WITH STAR
CENTER), #308
Company: U.S. Glass Co.
Years: 1926; 1956
Colors: crystal; crystal, green,
Plum, Citron
Items: 100+

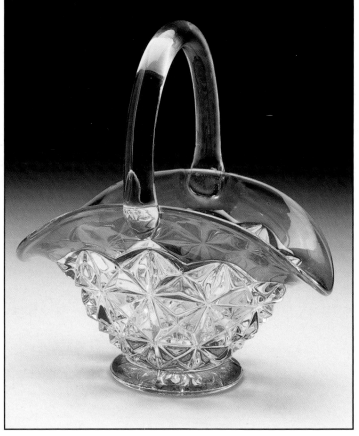

PATTERN NAME: WILLOW, #715
Company: Cambridge Glass Co.
Years: c. 1926
Colors: gold with green, gold
with light purple
Items: 15+

PATTERN NAME: WINDSOR
Company: Anchor Hocking
Glass Corp.
Years: 1946
Colors: Crystal, green,
ruby
Items: 4

PATTERN NAME: WINDSOR
Company: Indiana Glass Co.
Years: c. 1980s
Colors: Crystal, pink, blue
Items: 10

PATTERN NAME: WIRE SPIRAL OPTIC, #15
Company: U.S. Glass Co.
Years: c. 1926
Colors: crystal with green, blue,
          amber, lilac, and canary;
          crystal, amber; lilac
Items: 12

PATTERN NAME: WOODLAND ETCH, QUEEN
ANNE STEM,#7664
Company: Morgantown Glass Works
Years: c. 1931
Colors: azur, aqua marine, red, crystal
Items: 6

PATTERN NAME: "WOOLWORTH,"
"STIPPLED
GRAPE"
Company: Westmoreland
Years: c. 1930s; 1980s
Colors: green, pink
Items: 8

PATTERN NAME: YALE, #7684
Company: Morgantown Glass Works
Years: c. 1932
Colors: crystal with black, crystal
            with blue
Items: 10

PATTERN NAME: YESTERYEAR,
            LINE #1900
Company: Viking Glass Co.
Years: 1957
Colors: crystal, milk glass,
            amethyst, other
            colors

Anchor Hocking Glass Corp. Glassware Catalogs. Lancaster, OH: Anchor Hocking Glass Corp., 1941, 1942, 1949, 1959 – 60.

Archer, Margaret and Douglas. *Imperial Glass*. Paducah, KY: Collector Books, 1978.

Baker, Gary E, G. Eason Eige, Holly Hoover McCluskey, James S. Measell, Jane Shadel Spillman, Kenneth M. Wilson. *Wheeling Glass, 1829 – 1939, Collection of the Oglebay Institute Glass Museum*. Wheeling, WV: Oglebay Institute, 1994.

Barnett, Jerry. *Paden City, The Color Company*. Astoria, IL: Stevens Publishing Company, 1978.

Bennett, Harold & Judy. *The Cambridge Glass Book*. Des Moines, IA: Wallace- Homestead Book Co., 1970.

Bickenheuser, Fred. "Glass Notes...Manhattan." *Glass Review,* Vol. 10, No. 3, Mar., 1980, pgs. 12 – 13.

Bickenheuser, Fred. *Tiffin Glassmasters*. Grove City, OH: Glassmasters Publication, 1979.

—. *Tiffin Glassmasters, II*. Grove City, OH: Glassmasters Publication, 1981.

—. *Tiffin Glassmasters, III*. Grove City, OH: Glassmasters Publication, 1985.

Bones, Frances, ed. *Genuine Duncan, The Loveliest Glassware in America, Catalogue Reprints Years 1939 – 1951*. Fresno, TX: Frances Bones.

Bones, Frances. *The Book of Duncan Glass*. Des Moines, IA: Wallace-Homestead Co., 1973.

Bredehoft, Neila and Tom. *Hobbs, Brockunier & Co. Glass*. Paducah, KY: Collector Books, 1997.

—. *The Collector's Encyclopedia of Heisey Glass, 1925 – 1938*. Paducah, KY: Collector Books, 1993.

—. *Fifty Years of Collectible Glass, 1920 – 1970*. Dubuque, IA: Antique Trader Books, A Division of Landmark Specialty Publications, 1997.

Burkholder, John R. & D. Thomas O'Connor. *Kemple Glass, 1945 – 1970*. Marietta, OH: The Glass Press, Inc., dba Antique Publications, 1997.

Burns, Carl O. *Imperial Carnival Glass*. Paducah, KY: Collector Books, 1996.

Burns, Mary Louise. *Heisey's Glassware of Distinction*. Mesa, AZ: Triangle Books, 1974.

Canton Glass Company, Inc. *Glassware by Canton*. Marion, IN: Canton Glass Company, 1954.

Conder, Lyle, Ed. *Collector's Guide to Heisey's Glassware for Your Table*. Glass City, IN: L.W. Book Sales, 1984.

Dalzell Viking. An American Tradition in Glass Since 1884, 16 Page Catalogue. New Martinsville, WV: Dalzell-Viking.

Duncan & Miller Glass Co. Hand-Made Duncan, Catalogue No. 89 (Reprint). Washington, PA: Duncan & Miller Co., copyright pending by Richard Harold and Robert Roach.

Duncan & Miller, Inc. Genuine Duncan, Catalogue No. 77-1-43. Washington, PA: The Duncan & Miller Glass Co., 1943.

Duncan & Miller, Inc. Hand-made Duncan, Catalogue No. 93. Tiffin, OH: Duncan & Miller Division, U.S. Glass, Company, Inc.

Edwards, Bill & Mike Carwile. *Standard Encyclopedia of Pressed Glass, 1860 – 1930*. Paducah, KY: Collector Books, 1999.

Edwards, Bill. *Standard Encyclopedia of Opalescent Glass*. Paducah, KY: Collector Books, 1995.

Emanuele, Concetta, *Stems*. Sunol, CA: Olive Tree Publications, 1970.

Federal Glass Co. Federal Glassware - Quality You Can See, Catalog No. 56. Columbus, OH: Federal Glass Co.

Florence, Gene. Elegant Glassware of the Depression Era, 7th Ed. Paducah, KY: Collector Books, 1997.

Fostoria Glass Co. Eastern Price List Catalogues. Moundsville, WV: Fostoria, 1960, 1974, 1974 – 75, 1976 , 1978 & 1980.

Fostoria Glass Co. Fine Table Glassware. Moundsville, WV: Fostoria Glass Co., 1933.

Fostoria Glass Co. Fostoria, Fine Crystal and Colored Glassware, Cut, Etched and Plain, No. 2 Catalogue. Moundsville, WV: Fostoria Glass Co.

Fostoria Glass Company, 1901 Catalogue Reprint. Paducah, KY: Collector Books.

Gallagher, Jerry. *A Handbook of Old Morgantown Glass,* Vol. 1. Minneapolis, MN: Merit Printing, 1995.

Garrison, Myrna & Bob. *Imperial's Vintage Milk Glass,* Rev. 2nd Ed.. Arlington, TX: Collector's Loot, 1991.

H.C. Fry Glass Society. *The Collector's Encyclopedia of Fry Glassware*. Paducah, KY: Collector Books, 1990.

Hall, Linda F., ed. Reprints Seneca Glass Co. Catalogue No. 79 and No. 81. Morgantown, WV: Linda F. Hall.

Heacock, William, James Measell & Berry Wiggins. *Dugan/Diamond, The Story of Indiana, Pennsylvania, Glass*. Marietta, OH: Antique Publications, 1993.

Heacock, William. *The Glass Collector,* Issue No 3, Summer, 1982.

Heacock, William. *Victoria Colored Pattern Glass,* Bk. III. Marietta, OH: Richardson Printing Corp., 1976.

Heacock, William. *Encyclopedia of Victorian Colored Pattern Glass*. Marietta, OH: Antiques Publications, 1974.

—. *Opalescent Glass from A to Z*. Marietta, OH: Richardson Printing Corp. 1975.

—. *The Glass Collector,* ISS. 1. Marietta, OH: Peacock Publications, 1982.

—. *The Glass Collector,* ISS. 4. Marietta, OH: Peacock Publications, 1983.

—. *The Glass Collector,* ISS. 6. Marietta, OH: Peacock Publications, 1983.

—. *Fenton Glass, The 1980s Decade*. Marietta, OH: Glass Press, Inc. 1996.

—. *Fenton Glass, The First Twenty-Five Years*. Marietta, OH: Richardson Printing, 1978.

—. *Fenton Glass, The Second Twenty-Five Years*. Marietta, OH: O-Val Advertising Corp., 1980.

Heisey Glassware Pressed Ware Catalogue No. 109. Gas City, IN: L-W Promotions, 1974.

Hemminger, Ruth, Ed Goshe and Leslie Pina. *Tiffin Modern, Mid Century Art Glass*. Atglen, PA: Schiffer Publishing Ltd., 1997.

Higbee, Lola & Wayne. *Bryce, Higbee and J. B. Higbee Glass*. Marietta, OH: The Glass Press, Inc. dba Antique Publications, 1998.

Hinchliffe, Vel. "Depression Glass — or Is It Really Earlier," *Glass Review,* Vol 10, No. 9, Aug. and Sept. 1980 , pgs. 28 – 29 and pgs. 27 – 29 resp.

Imperial Glass Corp. *Handcrafted Imperial Glass*. Marietta, OH: Richardson Printing Corp., 1972.

Jenks, Bill, Jerry Luna & Darryl Reilly. *Identifying Pattern Glass Reproductions*. Radnor, PA: Wallace-Homestead Book Co., 1993.

Kerr, Ann. *Fostoria — An Identification & Value Guide of Pressed, Blown & Hand Molded Shapes*. Paducah, KY: Collector Books, 1994.

—. *Fostoria,* Vol. II. Paducah, KY: Collector Books, 1997.

King, W. L., Compiler. *Duncan & Miller Glass,* 2nd Ed. Venetia, PA: Victoria House Museum.

—. *Duncan & Miller Glass,* Sec. Ed. Venetia, PA: Victoria House Museum.

Koch, Nora, ed. *The Daze Past,* Compilation Mar. '71 – Dec. '75. Otisville, MI: Nora Koch, 1976.

Koch, Nora. *Reprint of 1916 Catalogue of Lead Blown Glassware Mfgd. by Bryce Brothers Company.* Otisville, MI: The Daze, 1984.

Kovar, Lorraine. *The Westmoreland Story, 1950 – 1984.* Marietta, OH: Antique Publications, 1991.

—. *Westmoreland Glass, 1888 – 1940,* Vol III. Marietta, OH: The Glass Press, Inc. dba

Krause, Gail. "Delightfully Duncan." *Rainbow Review Glass Journal,* Vol. 7, No. 10, Oct. 1977, pgs. 11 – 12.

—. *The Encyclopedia of Duncan Glass.* Hicksville, NY: Exposition Press, 1976.

Long, Milbra & Emily Seate. *Fostoria Tableware, 1924 – 1943.* Paducah, KY: Collector Books, 1999.

—. *Fostoria Tableware, 1944 – 1986.* Paducah, KY: Collector Books, 1999.

McCain, Mollie Helen. *The Collector's Encyclopedia of Pattern Glass.* Paducah, KY: Collector Books, 1998.

Measell, James & Don E. Smith. *Findlay Glass, The Glass Tableware Mfgs, 1886 – 1902.* Marietta, OH: Antique Publications, Inc., 1986.

Measell, James & W. C. "Red" Roetteis. *The L. G. Wright Glass Company.* Marietta, OH: The Glass Press, Inc. dba Antique Publications, 1997.

Measell, James, Ed. *Imperial Glass Encyclopedia,* Vol. I. Marietta, OH: The Glass Press, Inc., dba Antique Publications, 1995.

—. *Imperial Glass Encyclopedia,* Vol. II. Marietta, OH: The Glass Press, Inc. 1997.

Measell, James. *New Martinsville Glass, 1900 – 1944.* Marietta, OH: Antique Publications, 1994.

Metz, Alice Hulett. *Early American Pattern Glass.* Columbus, OH: Spencer-Walker Press, 1958.

—. *Much More Early American Pattern Glass,* Book II. Columbus, OH: Spencer-Walker Press, 1965.

Miller, Everett R. and Addie R. *The New Martinsville Glass Story Book II, 1920 – 1950.* Manchester, MI: Rymack Printing Company, 1975.

Nat'l Cambridge Collectors, Inc. *Genuine Handmade Cambridge, 1949 – 1953.* Paducah, KY: Collector Books, 1978.

—. *The Cambridge Glass Co., 1930 – 1934.* Paducah, KY: Collector Books, 1976.

National Cambridge Collectors, Inc. Reprint of 1940 Cambridge Glass Company Catalogue. Cambridge, OH: National Cambridge Collectors, Inc., 1995.

National Greentown Glass Assoc. *The D.C. Jenkins Glass Company Catalog.* Hillsdale, MI: Ferguson Communications, 1984.

Newbound, Betty & Bill. *Collector's Encyclopedia of Milk Glass.* Paducah, KY: Collector Books, 1995.

Nye, Mark. *Cambridge Stemware,* Sec. Ed. Brooklyn, MI: Mark A. Nye, 1994.

Page, Bob and Dale Frederiksen. *Crystal Stemware Identification Guide.* Paducah, KY: Collector Books.

Page, Bob and Dale Frederiksen. *A Collection of American Crystal.* Greensboro, NC: Page-Frederiksen Publishing Company, 1995.

Page, Bob. *Seneca Glass Co., 1891 – 1983.* Greensboro, NC: Page-Frederiksen Publishing Co., 1995.

—. *Tiffin is Forever.* Greensboro, NC: Page-Frederiksen Publishing Co., 1994.

Ream, Louise, Neila M., and Thomas H. Bredehoft. *Encyclopedia of Heisey Glassware,* Vol. 1. Newark, OH: Heisey Collectors of America, Inc., 1977.

Schaeffer, Barbara and Vel Hinchliffe. "What's in a Name?," #162 and #124 Pattern. *Glass Review,* Vol. 10, No. 4, April, 1980, pgs. 22-23.

Scott, Virginia. "Looking through the Ads with... No. 23. Westmoreland's "Swirl and Ball." *Rainbow Review Glass Journal,* Vol. 5, No. 7, July, 1975, pgs. 14 & 15.

Seneca Glass Co. Catalogue No. 73. Morgantown, WV: Seneca Glass Co.

Sferrazza, Julie. *Farber Brothers, Krome Kraft.* Marietta, OH: Antique Publications, 1988.

Shaeffer, Barbara, ed. *Rainbow Review Glass Journal,* Vol. 7, No. 5. Costa Mesa, CA: 1977.

—. *Rainbow Review Glass Journal,* Vol. 7, No. 11, Nov. 1977, pg. 24.

Shumpert, Gwen. "Gwen's Glassline." *Glass Review,* Vol 8., No. 7, July, 1978, pg. 6.

Smith, Bill and Phyllis. *Cambridge Glass, 1927 –1929.* Springfield, OH: 1986.

Stout, Sandra McPhee. *The Complete Book of McKee.* N. Kansas City, KS: The Trojan Press, 1972.

Teal, Ron, Sr. *Albany Glass, Model Flint Glass Co. of Albany, IN.* Marietta, OH: The Glass Press, Inc. dba Antique Publications, 1997.

Tiara Exclusives Catalogue, Eaton, IN: Colony Printing and Labeling, Inc., 1985.

Viking Glass Company. Treasured American Glass. New Martinsville, WV: Viking Glass Company.

Vogel, Clarence W. *Heisey's First Ten Years...1896 – 1905.* Plymouth, OH: Heisey Publications, 1969.

—. *Heisey on Parade.* Lombard, IL: Wallace-Homestead, 1985.

—. *Heisey's Art and Colored Glass, 1922 – 1942.* Plymouth, OH: Heisey Publications, 1970.

—. *Heisey's Colonial Years...1906 – 1922.* Plymouth, OH: Heisey Publications, 1969.

—. *Heisey's Early and Late Years, 1896 – 1958.* Plymouth, OH: Heisey Publications, 1971.

Walker, Mary, Lyle and Lynn. *The Cambridge Glass Co.,* Book I. New Concord, OH: Lyle L. Walker, 1970.

—. *The Cambridge Glass Co.* Newark, OH: Spencer Walker Press, 1974.

Walker, William P. "Those Confusing Woodland Scenes," *Glass Collector's Digest,* Vol XI, No. 6., May, 1998, pgs. 20 – 27.

Weatherman, Hazel Marie. *Colored Glassware of the Depression Era 2.* Springfield, MO: Weatherman Glassbooks, 1974.

—. *Fostoria, Its First Fifty Years.* Springfield, MO: The Weathermans, 1979.

Westmoreland Glass Co. "Gifts of Heritage" Our 90th Year—1889 – 1979, 1979 Consumer Catalogue, Grapeville, PA: Westmoreland Glass Co., 1979.

Westmoreland Glass Co. 1974 Supplement. Marietta, OH: Richardson Printing Corp., 1974.

Westmoreland Glass Co. Catalogue No. 75. Grapeville, PA: Westmoreland Glass Co., 1964.

Westmoreland Glass Co. Westmoreland...where pride and excellence in craftsmanship is a tradition. Grapeville, PA: Westmoreland Glass Co., 1971.

Whitmyer, Margaret & Kenn. *Fenton Art Glass, 1907 – 1939.* Paducah, KY: Collector Books, 1996.

Wilson, Charles West. *Westmoreland Glass.* Paducah, KY: Collector Books, 1996.

Wilson, Jack D. *Phoenix and Consolidated Art Glass: 1926 – 1980.* Marietta, OH: Antique Publications, 1996.

Ziegler, Roserita. "Researching with...Priscilla, Fenton & L. G. Wright Co." *Glass Review,* Vol. 10, Nov. 1980, pgs. 24 – 26.

Company Index

Company Index

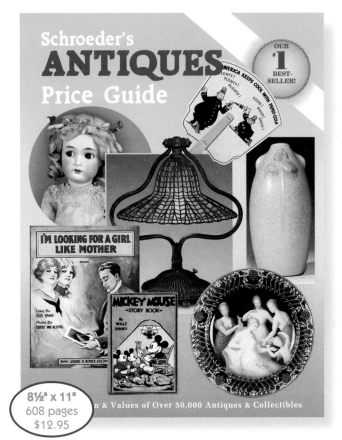